LETTERS TO A NEW DEVELOPER

WHAT I WISH I HAD KNOWN WHEN STARTING MY DEVELOPMENT CAREER

Dan Moore

Apress®

Letters to a New Developer: What I Wish I Had Known When Starting my Development Career

Dan Moore
Boulder, CO, USA

ISBN-13 (pbk): 978-1-4842-6073-9   ISBN-13 (electronic): 978-1-4842-6074-6
https://doi.org/10.1007/978-1-4842-6074-6

Managing Director, Apress Media LLC: Welmoed Spahr
Acquisitions Editor: Louise Corrigan
Development Editor: James Markham
Coordinating Editor: Nancy Chen

Cover designed by eStudioCalamar

Distributed to the book trade worldwide by Springer Science+Business Media New York, 1 New York Plaza, New York, NY 100043. Phone 1-800-SPRINGER, fax (201) 348-4505, e-mail orders-ny@springer-sbm.com, or visit www.springeronline.com. Apress Media, LLC is a California LLC and the sole member (owner) is Springer Science + Business Media Finance Inc (SSBM Finance Inc). SSBM Finance Inc is a **Delaware** corporation.

For information on translations, please e-mail rights@apress.com, or visit http://www.apress.com/rights-permissions.

Apress titles may be purchased in bulk for academic, corporate, or promotional use. eBook versions and licenses are also available for most titles. For more information, reference our Print and eBook Bulk Sales web page at http://www.apress.com/bulk-sales.

Any source code or other supplementary material referenced by the author in this book is available to readers on GitHub via the book's product page, located at www.apress.com/9781484260739. For more detailed information, please visit http://www.apress.com/source-code.

Printed on acid-free paper

To my ladies:
Pam, Charlotte, and Lucy

Contents

About the Author

 **Dan Moore** has over 20 years of experience as a developer. His roles have included employee, contractor, community member, engineering manager, and CTO. He currently leads developer advocacy at FusionAuth, a Denver company, building software to handle authentication, authorization, and user management for any app. In 2018, Dan started a blog exclusively focused on helping new developers "level up" and has published over 150 posts to help them improve their skills and avoid common mistakes. He resides in Boulder, CO. You can find him on Twitter at @mooreds.

Acknowledgments

Often, I recall a comic from Nathan Pyle. In it a customer is waiting in a shop; the shopkeeper asks "Have you been helped?" And the customer answers "By so many people my entire life."

I, too, have been helped by so many people in my life, my career, and during the writing of this book. My heart overflows with gratitude.

Thank you to all the new developers I've talked with and been educated by. Whether I met you at a meetup, a conference, or online, you've taught me so much.

To my editors at Apress, Louise Corrigan, Nancy Chen, and Jim Markham: thanks for guiding me through this experience.

Thanks to my guest letter writers, who shared their experience, time, and wisdom. I'd especially like to thank those who allowed me to use their letters in this book: Allan Wintersieck, Brooke Kuhlmann, Cara Borenstein, Cierra Nease, Dave Mayer, Jeff Beard, John Obelenus, Josh Thompson, Kim Schlesinger, Mark Sawers, Morgan Whaley, Noel Worden, Rick Manelius, Rishi Malik, Rylan Bowers, and Zach Turner.

The chapter reviewers have my gratitude as well. You challenged my ideas and sharpened my thoughts. I'll lay claim to my mistakes, though. Thanks to Andy Pai, Brian Timoney, Corey Snipes, Emerson Loustau, Ian Sprod, Kendall Miller, Kim Schlesinger, Marty Haught, Mike Gehard, Miles Matthias, Ned McClain, Pam Moore, Rylan Bowers, and Steve Ham.

So many of the skills required to be a developer are learned on the job. I've been taught so much by my colleagues, managers, and reports. I'd like to acknowledge four of my bosses in particular.

Bryan Buus, who took a call from a college senior during frenetic preparations for the Kentucky Derby. Thank you for introducing that new developer to the XOR family.

By watching Anthony Francavilla and Lane Horning, my eyes were opened to the power, strength, and fragility of business partnerships. I also learned about the connection between deep business domain knowledge and great software. Lane also gave me my first swing at engineering management.

Acknowledgments

My thanks to Ashley Colpaart, who shared her vision with me and took me along on an adventure. Together we survived the crucible of starting a boot-strapped software business.

I also want to thank my family for encouraging and supporting me throughout my career. Special shout-out to my parents for forcing me to work in their business as a middle schooler, where I first saw the power of software to alleviate human toil.

Thank you to Charlotte and Lucy for giving up your dad on weekends and weeknights as I worked on this book. I'm thrilled to be your father.

Finally, thank you to my wife, Pam. She's my biggest supporter. She gave me the time to write this and pushed me to start when I hesitated. I love you.

Introduction

This book is full of lessons I've learned. I wrote it to help new developers like you. When I started developing software, I had many assumptions. Over the last two decades of working in companies both big and small, alongside tens of thousands of employees and as a startup cofounder, I saw how my assumptions were incorrect.

During that time, I also was introduced to specialties and disciplines that I never imagined were part of software development, and my eyes were opened further.

It was not always easy to learn. I made missteps. I was humbled by teammates, managers, and clients. More than once, I had to sit down at the computer and grind.

I wrote this book to share all this with you.

However, this is not a book about a certain technology or a specialized program you might use. Sure, there is an entire chapter about tools a developer should eventually master, but specific technologies are beside the point. If you are looking for a book to help you understand the latest JavaScript framework, microservices architecture, or DevOps platform (or, for the ambitious, all three!), please buy a different book.

This book is, instead, about principles and practices that never go out of style. These were germane two decades ago and will be relevant far into the future. A lot of what I'll cover are called "soft skills," but they're pretty hard to learn. As far as I know, no college or bootcamp offers "How to Make Mistakes 101." It was easier for me to learn how to program a computer than how to collaborate with a team. Computers get faster every year, but people change every day. And they matter. Software exists only because humans shape it, need it, and pay for it.

Among other topics, this book includes practices to help you level up as a developer, tools to learn, the right way to ask questions, and the role of community in software development.

Over many years, I have learned what it takes to be a professional software developer. While I think anybody working in software can benefit from this book, I wrote it for three audiences: new developers, people considering software development as a career, and mentors.

For new developers

You are new to the software development job market. Perhaps you have completed a bootcamp or college degree. You may refer to yourself as an entry-level or junior engineer.

While everyone's background and skills growth happens at different speeds, new developers generally have less than five years of professional experience. Many new developers are worried about their abilities, don't feel welcome, and have a difficult time finding that first job.

But as an industry, we *need* more new developers. There are so many problems with which software can help. Companies want experienced engineers, but all the senior developers I know started out as new developers. A senior engineer is just a new engineer seasoned with gaffes, education, and time.

For new developers, this book will help you avoid missteps I've made. It also introduces you to disciplines beyond coding critical to success. While programming is crucial for any software product or service, there is much more required to deliver an application.

For anyone considering software development

If you're not sure if software engineering is right for you, this book offers perspectives on how to succeed.

I've intentionally kept the barriers to the layperson low with limited technical jargon. Only a few technologies are discussed, and those sections can be skipped. If you are thinking about becoming a developer, I'd recommend buying this book *and* a book about programming.

Giving a computer commands that it can execute is an important skill for any software developer. But software engineering is so much more. You must know what to build, how to work with your team, and how to maintain your systems.

For mentors

If you are mentoring a new developer, this book can serve as a discussion guide. Because each chapter has letters approaching a theme from different angles, you and your mentee will find it useful for focused mentoring sessions.

As an experienced developer, you'll of course bring your own insights and experience to each topic, from your debugging process to the value of an online community for continuous learning.

And, of course, you may have had a different experience than what I share. Such contrasts are a jumping-off point to discuss the diversity available in a software development career.

Format

This book is a conversation.

Each chapter consists of letters around a theme, written from me to you. This format allows me to approach a topic from different perspectives. At the same time, each letter is easy to read in a single sitting. I read before bed and wanted to write a software book that would neither keep you up nor put you to sleep.

To give the reader a broader view, I have invited other engineers and professionals, from recent bootcamp graduates to CTOs, to contribute their viewpoints. You'll see their letters interspersed among mine, signed by the author.

Thank you

Thank you very much for giving me your attention and time. The lessons from this book will accelerate your software development career. You will learn how to make decisions, timeless tools, and who should manage your career (spoiler alert, it's on you).

In reading this book, you'll learn what I did wrong. And what I did right. You'll make mistakes—trust me, I know! But you will make fewer errors than I did.

Finally, *welcome*!

Welcome to the software development world. You belong here. Just like the real world, it's delightful and dizzying, frustrating and fantastic, grungy and gorgeous.

Welcome, new developer. Welcome.

Your First Month

Your first month is a time of great promise. You are joining a company and team who are excited to have you. You represent success in a long arduous hiring process.

Everything is new for both you and your employer. There's a lot to share and learn for both parties.

Enjoy.

There are no adults in the room

Dear new developer,

When I started working, I was shocked to learn that there are no adults in the room.

I say this not to denigrate your fellow employees, working hard to make the company successful. Rather, I'm saying no one knows it all. Everyone is doing the best they can with their limited information and understanding; well, most people—there are occasionally bad actors.

If you join a company expecting to be handed work on a platter, expecting someone knows exactly how to do that work, the way that a college professor knows how to teach physics 101, you will be disappointed. Your coworkers are usually trying to stay one step ahead of the customer.

© Dan Moore 2020

D. Moore, *Letters to a New Developer*, https://doi.org/10.1007/978-1-4842-6074-6_1

There are sometimes domain and process experts at a company, but I've only worked at one organization where someone truly understood the entire business. And even at that job, the future was unknown, and there was experimentation around new programs. "Hmmm, will that work? Let's try it and find out."

The software industry isn't alone in this lack of clockwork precision, by the way. I've talked with employees in other sectors. Never met someone who worked at a perfectly run organization. Even in places where stakes are life and death, like hospitals, there's chaos and uncertainty.

So, once you are hired and thrust into ambiguous situations, you can choose how you think about them.

- *It's a problem*—Oh my god, no one knows what the heck is going on. What kind of place is this?

- *What an opportunity!*—Excellent, I can see that folks are grappling with interesting problems and need help. Let me put my nose to the grindstone and see how I can assist.

You'll be happier, more productive, and a more valuable team member if you choose the second line of thought.

Of course, there are uncertainties that you shouldn't accept, such as anything that could damage your health or ethics. But it was empowering to me when I realized there were no adults in the room with all the answers.

Just people trying to do their best.

Sincerely,

Dan

Onboarding

Dear new developer,

At every full-time job I've ever had, there was an onboarding process. As a developer, there are typically two types: HR and company orientation and technology and process training.

Onboarding is your first chance to interact with the company as an employee. Companies want to help new hires navigate their jobs' invisible societal structures. This process will help you succeed, but it's often a firehose of information.

During the HR and company orientation, make sure you understand the myriad ways that you and the company will interact. This includes items such as:

- Your salary
- How you will be paid
- Health benefits
- Employment agreements
- Retirement accounts
- How to interact with other departments and teams
- Bonuses
- Company meetings
- How to request vacation
- When raises or reviews are scheduled

This onboarding should cover basically everything except the actual work you were hired to do.

Make sure you understand this information because it won't be systematically presented to you again and can affect your job satisfaction. In some cases, such as a noncompete, it will influence your future employment choices. If you have questions about this material, email is a great way to get them answered; when the exchange is over email, you have it for reference in the future. If you feel more comfortable having this conversation face to face, follow up in writing. Consider saying something like "I just wanted to make sure I was clear about our conversation. It's my understanding that...".

There may be an employee handbook, but maybe not; it depends on the size of the company and of the HR department. There may also be a wiki or documents on a shared drive, which you can review as well.

The technology and process onboarding, on the other hand, is all about enabling you to be an effective developer and team member. It should include:

- Who can you ask questions of?
- What is the best way to ask questions? Batch them up? Post to chat? Schedule a meeting?
- How long should you work on a problem that has you blocked? If you can't make forward progress, how long before you should ask for help?
- How do you communicate progress?
- How do you set up your local development environment on your own computer to start working on code?

- How does code you write get to production? Is continuous integration or deployment set up? What does the release cycle look like? Who, whether a single person or a team, owns releases?

- Where will you get direction from? A ticketing system or issue tracker? Your manager? Your team lead? The product owner?

- How will you know when you're done with a task? Is it when it is shipped to production? When a product owner approves it? Some other milestone?

The first month is all about getting up to speed in the organization's environment. Formal onboarding accelerates your ability to dig in, start adding value, and help the team achieve its goals.

What should you do if there is not a formal onboarding process? If you don't have a formal HR or company onboarding, you'll want written answers to your questions about how to interact with the company. However, even small companies I've joined have a formal process. Since a lack of one has legal consequences for the organization, only very small companies don't have one.

If there is not a formal technology onboarding, keep notes and start a document. You'll be helping future developers who join your team. This can be as simple as starting a wiki page.

An onboarding is usually your first interaction with the company as an employee. Take the opportunity to learn as much as you can, both about how the organization works and how to do your job as a developer.

Sincerely,

Dan

Overindex

Dear new developer,

It is unfortunate, but first impressions matter. Like many other jobs, success in software development requires working with other people. Therefore, bring your best self to work for the first month of any job. That doesn't mean you can check out later, but in the first month, you should stand out.

Here are some ways to stand out:

- Arrive a bit early every day.

- Say what you are going to do. Do what you say.

- Do extra research. When you have a question, don't just blurt it out. Instead see if it has been answered (search the wiki, search the chat).

- When you get an answer to a question, record that information for other team members' use.

- Volunteer to take on the extra work (but not too much—don't set yourself up as a punching bag).

- Own your mistakes. However, don't beat yourself up when they happen.

- Don't make the same mistake twice.

- Be unfailingly polite and professional.

- Ask for some of your manager's time to make sure you and they are on the same page regarding your goals. How often should you check in and report progress? I don't know, it differs with every manager. So, ask.

- Write documentation to make the next hire's life easier.

Once you have the reputation of being a hard, smart worker, it will follow you. After a month or two, you can ease off a bit—partly because you will have that standing and partly because you'll understand the job better. You'll be able to continue to perform your duties effectively with less effort.

When you first join an organization, everyone is excited. If you can overindex and achieve 105% or 110% of what they expect of you, team members will remain enthusiastic. However, if you deliver "only" 90% of what they expected, the excitement might fade.

First impressions last for years. Your reputation will follow you beyond the organization. Choose wisely.

Sincerely,

Dan

Work through the trepidation

Dear new developer,

I remember the first month of my first job. Not a pleasant memory. I wasn't sure who was who, what was what, or even sometimes why I was doing what I was doing. Even after onboarding, I was often confused. It was hard to find tasks I could do that helped my team. I wasn't sure what words and acronyms meant, even ones that people used offhandedly like "API". I'd read and reread instructions, fearful that I wasn't "doing it right."

Every day was a struggle.

Eventually, I learned my way around—around the codebase, around the organization, around my tools, around the team.

And everything got better. After a few weeks, I became more confident and able to help the team. We shipped software. Eventually, I even wrote best practices documentation about version control practices, sharing knowledge throughout the company.

And then I switched jobs. It happened again. The trepidation, I mean.

It was a bit easier because I had my previous experience to draw on. I knew the fear and uncertainty would pass. But I still needed to learn so much to be effective at job #2.

Eventually, things got better. Again, I learned my way around.

And then I switched jobs. It happened again. The trepidation, I mean.

See a pattern?

For every job I have ever had, the first month was tough. There's a lot you don't know, and worse, there are things you don't know that you don't know. Sometimes you'll be hired into a company that is moving fast. In that case, you may have a hard time even finding someone to answer your questions.

There's no quick fix, but there is a solution: recognize you will feel this trepidation. Put your head down and do the work. Take each day one at a time and celebrate your successes. Here are some achievements to celebrate:

- "Today, I learned how to deploy to our QA environment."
- "Today, I fixed two bugs and discovered a third."
- "Today, we were in a meeting and I shared a meaningful comment."
- "Today I closed one ticket."
- "Today, I figured out who the Docker experts in the company are."

Keep on working. And, soon enough, you'll break through and find your way. I promise.

Sincerely,

Dan

How to excel at your job

Dear new developer,

I think that there are only four things you need to do to be a great new developer:

- *Say what you are going to do, then do it*—Communicate what you are working on. You can do this synchronously (face-to-face communication or a chat message) or implicitly (moving cards on your task tracking system or in an email). Keep other people, who will have a better idea of the big picture, in the loop. Oh, and then you must **do** the work.

- *Ask questions*—Don't be afraid of looking dumb. Do some research before you ask as that often will answer your question, but don't spin your wheels. Ask meta-questions such as "Who is the best person to ask this question?" or "How much time should I spend investigating on my own before asking a question?" This will help you do the work.

- *Don't make the same mistake twice*—Learn from those you do make. Write down what you did wrong and how you plan to avoid doing it in the future. If it is a common mistake, share your documentation with the team. This will help you do the work better in the future.

- *Show up consistently*—Be a bit better every day. Keep your spirits up by remembering how far you've come. Put in the time. Sometimes you just have to grind. To do the work. (Is there an echo in here?)

Do these things, and you will stand out as a new developer.

Why? It's sad to say, but there are many developers who aren't very good. I've seen a few in my time. I'm not sure if they weren't good because they were burned out, didn't care, didn't have the skill set or the desire to learn, or were just in it for the money.

I've also seen developers get complacent, which is a foolish thing to do in this day and age. It's also a luxury that most new developers do not have. You don't need to be an expert in every new technology, but you do need to keep your skills up to date.

You don't have to be brilliant to stand out. You do have to be good and consistent. And you must do the work (there it is again!).

Focus on these four items, especially during your first month, and you'll gain a reputation as a delight to work with. This reputation will follow you for years. People will offer you opportunities, return your phone calls, and help you find jobs and advise you.

Sincerely,

Dan

Learn your team

Dear new developer,

You will learn many things during your first month on the job—how to deploy the software, coding conventions, homegrown frameworks, good places for lunch.

But the most important thing you can pick up in your first few weeks at a job is team dynamics. Even if you are the only technical person in the company (which I suggest you avoid), you will still have coworkers who use or run software systems. Someone has to tell you what to do. Someone has to tell you what customers you serve.

You will be operating in a team environment, and you'll need to both assist the team and lean on the team when you need help. The best way to get what you need is to get to know your coworkers. When you know team members, you'll both understand who to approach with a given problem and how to relate to them during tense times. To whom would you rather lend a hand, a stranger or someone who has taken the time to get to know you?

Here are some concrete tips for learning team members and dynamics:

- *Learn everyone's name*—When I'm meeting someone new, I like to repeat back their name as soon as possible to reinforce it in my mind. Usually, I'll ask a question: "So, Ahmed, what new technologies are you excited about?" Other ways include taking written notes or associating the name with a relevant interesting fact. Whatever works.

- *Learn each person's area of responsibility*—Almost everyone I've met loves to talk about themselves. Over the course of your first month, ask everyone you meet what they do. What challenges do they face? What excites them about the project and the company?

- *Go out to lunch*—At my first job, I saved money by bringing my own lunch. That is a smart financial move, but a dumb career move. Lunches help teams build cohesion. You don't have to break your budget by going out every day but join a few times a week. Consider buying lunch an investment in your career that will pay dividends. At shared meals, you learn more about your coworkers, including their personal lives, interests, and hobbies.

- *Say yes to other social activities if you can*—The first month is when people will be most welcoming and so may invite you out. Don't do anything you feel uncomfortable with or can't afford, of course.

- *If you work in a remote team, ask your manager how you can get to know other people*—Depending on the maturity of your organization, they may have a formal process, but you can also do random video calls.

In my experience, personal dynamics are almost never laid out for you when you join a team. You may get pointed to "Jane, who is an expert in system XYZ," but that's about it. You'll have to play detective.

Note who talks at meetings, who does not, and who isn't invited to the meetings at all. Pay attention to whose opinions are dismissed and whose are respected (but make your own decisions about the wisdom of those choices). See who hangs out with each other at social events and who drops funny gifs in the company chat.

This knowledge will help you know who to seek out when you need help, whether that is about the history of a certain component, how to build subsystem XYZ (I suggest Jane), or how to request assistance from another department.

Sincerely,

Dan

How to read code

Dear new developer,

Reading code is more common than writing code. In your first month of work, you'll be reading a lot of code as you try to understand new systems you'll be working with. Some developers even say, "don't trust any documentation, read the code," though I consider that a radical position.

But how can you effectively read code?

First, you need to understand the syntax of the language (or languages). How are methods or functions called? How do you define a variable? How is the code modularized? This is the first step, just like learning the letters of the alphabet.

Then you want to start to understand the meaning of the code. Most systems are too big to hold entirely in any one person's head, so pick a part to dig into. Trace the flow of data through the system. Start from whatever event kicks off code (a user interaction, a file being placed somewhere, an external sensor firing) and follow the data flow. Don't get distracted; if you see something you'd like to learn more about but it is not in the data flow you are currently examining, jot down a note and come back to it later. This activity is analogous to learning to read.

I also find it useful to understand the architecture of the system. This is the "boxes and arrows" drawing which relates the pieces of a system together. Having this big picture won't help you with the details of the code you're reading, but I find it helpful when other subsystems or components are referenced. This is analogous to the "Cliff's Notes" of a book.

As you continue on your software engineering path, you'll need to move between these levels of abstraction. Like reading a human language, the more you do it, the better you'll be. Eventually, you will gain intuition around the system.

But that'll take a lot more than a month.

Sincerely,

Dan

Learn about personal finance

Dear new developer,

If you have a software development job, you're probably making pretty good money. I know when I started my first job, I was making more money than I ever had before. I had an annual salary of $42,000, in 1999 (which is $65,250 in 2020 dollars).

Man, it felt good to just buy what I wanted to buy and not worry about it.

One financially smart thing that I did at that first job was to set up my 401k contribution. Shockingly, it's far better to save for 10 years starting from age 25 than for 30 years starting from age 35. It's all thanks to the magic of compound interest.

Let's illustrate this point with some simplifying assumptions:

- You contribute $5000 every year to your retirement savings on January 1.

- Your savings grow tax-free (in a 401k or IRA or similar account).

- The annual rate of return including fees is 7%.

- You receive your gains on December 31; for example, on December 31 of the first year you contribute, you have $5000*0.07 + $5000, so $5350 in your account.

As you can see in Figure 1-1, the person who saved for 10 years starting at age 25, contributing $50,000, will have approximately $560,000 in savings at age 65. If instead you start at age 35 and save for 30 years, contributing $150,000, you will end up with approximately $505,000. That's a difference of about $55,000 at age 65, even though the person who started at 35 contributed $100,000 more of their earned income.

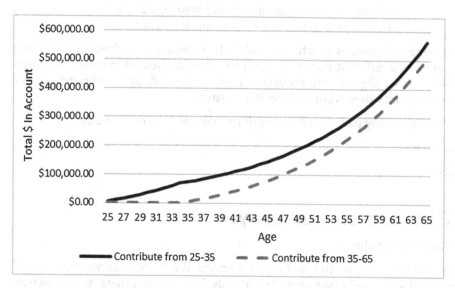

Figure 1-1. The magic of compound interest

Take advantage of time and put money away early.

You will be well served by getting smart about personal finance. Here are books that shaped my financial thinking:

- *A Random Walk Down Wall Street*—This book convinced me that index funds were the best way to buy stocks and bonds and that trying to beat the market is a fool's errand.

- *Are You a Stock or a Bond?*—This book taught me that you should save differently based on the kind of job you have. Do you have a riskier job, at a startup or in a cyclical industry? Save more in bonds. Shift your investment portfolio based on the risk of your income.

- *Your Money or Your Life*—This book made me think about money as life energy, which made me more conscious of how I spent it. The advice on investing is a bit conservative for me, however.

- *Personal Finance for Dummies*—A nuts and bolts discussion of investment opportunities and how to build a budget. This book is great for personal finance basics.

Personally, I saved as much as I could when I was a new developer, but you may make a different choice. I have a friend who invested in solar companies because that aligned with his values. I have other colleagues who didn't start investing until they were in their 30s or later.

There are many paths. Learn enough to make an informed choice.

Sincerely,

Dan

Take care of your body

Dear new developer,

I'm not a doctor, so this isn't medical advice. But from experience, I can tell you that you should take care of your body. This includes things that all people should do:

- Get good sleep.

- Exercise regularly.

- Schedule regular checkups with your doctor, dentist, and other health-care providers.

But it also includes concerns specific to desk jockeys such as:

- Walk away from your desk periodically.
- Consider a standing desk.
- Look 20 feet away from your monitor every 20 minutes for 20 seconds.[1]

There are some items that are specific to software engineers:

- Use as large a monitor as possible.
- Change the font on your screen to be easy on your eyes.
- Don't work crazy hours.
- Use an ergonomic keyboard.

Some of these items require the cooperation of your employer. Ask for what you need, as keeping you healthy is in the interests of both parties. You might not get that 48-inch monitor, but if you don't ask, you surely won't.

Whatever you do, listen to your body. Take regular breaks. Buy the equipment you need, even if you must spend your own money.

When I was young, my body seemed to be an endless resource, capable of enduring anything.

From where I stand now, I can tell you with authority: it is not.

Sincerely,

Dan

In conclusion

In the first month of your job, you'll be drinking from the firehose. You will be getting up to speed on the technologies and specific implementation details of the systems you're working on. You'll also be trying to navigate the cultural norms of your new workplace.

This is exhausting labor. Make sure you allow yourself some slack, both in terms of how quickly you come up to speed and what you try to commit to outside of work.

But make sure you put in the time and the effort, too. This is no time to slack. First impressions matter.

---

[1] As recommended by the American Academy of Ophthalmology: www.aao.org/eye-health/tips-prevention/computer-usage

Questions

Questions are part of software development. There is so much on the job training, and the field is young. The first electronic computer was built in 1945, so general-purpose programmable computers and the software that runs them haven't been around for long.

Sometimes you'll be forced to make technical decisions without understanding everything. Asking the right questions can help you make these kinds of decisions in the least bad way possible.

As a new developer, make sure you understand how and when to ask questions. Asking great questions is as much about research before and listening to the answer after as it is about the content of your query.

Ask ~~smart~~ prepared questions

Dear new developer,

First, there are no dumb questions.

But there are unprepared ones.

The closer you are to someone, the more you can ask a question off the cuff. For example, if you are asking a peer how to connect to the database, you can expect an answer. However, if you look around, you may find the answer without even asking your colleagues; this is often the quickest way to solve your problem.

© Dan Moore 2020

D. Moore, *Letters to a New Developer*, https://doi.org/10.1007/978-1-4842-6074-6_2

But asking someone on the Internet the same question: "how do I connect to the database?", will probably result in silence on their part and frustration on yours. Why? They have neither the context nor the connection to you which your coworker does. You must provide them with both.

The best way to prepare is to write up the question in enough detail that you'd feel comfortable posting it on a question and answer site like Stack Overflow.

Here are the benefits of research when preparing to ask a question:

- You may find the answer yourself, perhaps documented in an internal wiki, the chat system, or on the Internet. Awesome! You just saved yourself time, learned a new resource, and didn't interrupt anybody.

- You clarify the question. When you write, you are forced to make the implicit explicit. How does the problem arise, exactly? Where? When? All of this is helpful for anyone trying to answer your question.

- Documenting the exact steps to replicate your question often suggests additional things to try: "ah, so I didn't investigate upgrading that library, I should try that."

Look at both internal company resources and the wider Internet when researching your question.

A wiki or a README in a source code repository can have what you need. Another internal resource is implicitly built documentation, such as an email list, commit log, or past chat. Source code can help answer a question too.

Helpful sections of the Internet include:

- Question and answer sites like Stack Overflow and the other Stack Exchange sites

- Internet-accessible forums

- Mailing lists, which usually have web-accessible archives

- Slacks and Facebook groups, where there's a lot of content that is not indexed by web search engines like Google

- IRC channels, often hosted by freenode

- Software issue trackers at GitHub, GitLab, or elsewhere

- YouTube and other video sites

All are fair game for your research. I typically start by using Google to search for specific terms. But be aware, as noted, some of these resources aren't available to search engines—you'll need to know about a Slack's existence before you can search it for the answer to your question.

By the way, the ability to search the Internet for answers is one reason for using commonplace technology—the resources available for a popular language framework typically dwarf the documentation available for a homegrown solution. This is a reason to avoid building custom frameworks whenever possible.

There's a trade-off in doing research, of course. Doing this research properly is time-consuming and may be frustrating. I always recommend asking more experienced peers how much time to spend doing research. If the project is on a tight timeline, it may be better to ask a less prepared question more quickly. This is especially true if you are asking a team member.

In a meta way, be prepared to ask questions to determine how much time to spend preparing to ask questions.

Side note: Asking where the copier is or what's a good lunch joint is *technically* a question, but not what I'm writing about.

Sincerely,

Dan

How to ask a question on the Internet

Dear new developer,

When you encounter a bug that stumps you, it's natural to ask questions of communities on the Internet. After all, there are a lot of smart people out there. If you ask a question, make sure you do it well. Maximize your chances of having your question answered: ask it in the clearest, most concise way possible.

Please realize that the people in these communities aren't usually paid to answer your questions. No matter how frustrated you are, or how broken something is, be kind and polite. Being rude will ensure your question is ignored.

Here's a poorly worded question: "I can't figure out why my nodejs application won't start. Can anyone help me?" This question falls short because:

- It isn't precise. What does "won't start" mean?

- It puts most of the effort on the question answerer to replicate your situation, either by guessing or asking you for more details.

- You haven't shown any effort. How have you tried to solve the issue? We don't know.

Contrast the preceding question with this question:

> "I can't figure out why my nodejs application won't start. I'm using nodejs version 12.3 and express v4.1. I'm running on the latest macOS but have also tested on Ubuntu 20.04.
>
> When I start the application by running "node server/index.js", I see this message in the log files: EADDRINUSE, Address already in use
>
> But when I use netstat to look for anything bound to port 3000, which is what my node server should be attaching to, I don't see anything.
>
> You can see a simplified version of the source code at http://github.com/username/brokennode/ if you'd like to take a look.
>
> I've Googled around for the error message and haven't found anything useful. Can anyone help me? Thanks in advance."

Anyone can tell that the asker has put in effort to answer the question on their own, including searching the Web and reviewing logs. A possible answerer can easily download the code and try it. It is clear exactly what "the app won't start" means.

Here are some tips for asking a good question:

- Specify your problem in detail. If it's a bug, spend the time to narrow it down to the smallest set of replication steps. Include code or a test if you can. If it is a question, narrow the scope of the question as much as possible.

- Show you've done your research. This includes searches; links to pertinent issues, videos, or posts; and any logs or output around the issue. Make sure you remove sensitive information from the logs.

- Follow up if you have not found an answer. Wait for a day or so and follow up with additional information if you haven't found a solution. You've probably been doing additional research or troubleshooting, so share it.

- Express gratitude. If someone takes the time to answer your question, or even to clarify a point, make sure to thank them.

If you do get an answer to a question, whether through your own research, someone's assistance, or a combination, respond to your question with the answer. It's frustrating to find a post on the Internet where one's exact question has been asked, but never answered. Close the loop.

It's not easy to take the time to prepare a good question. I have been a new developer under pressure. I've seen many frustratingly vague questions on the Internet. I understand your desire to get your problem solved as soon as possible.

Again, it's easy to forget that the folks helping you are:

- Real people
- Not getting paid by you

No matter how obvious the bug seems, or how much it is impacting you, treat people helping you kindly. Every time you ask a question on the Internet, you are tasking a set of volunteers.

Treat them right.

Sincerely,

Dan

Don't be afraid to ask questions

Noel Worden *started his career as a photographer, shifted gears to become a cabinetmaker, then graduated from the coding bootcamp Bloc. He is currently working as a software engineer for MojoTech in Boulder, Colorado.*

Dear new developer,

Don't be afraid to ask questions. It can be stressful and humbling to reach out and ask a question, but it can be the best way to stop spinning your wheels and make progress. It's stressful because as a new developer you are trying to prove yourself to your peers and superiors. It's humbling because you are admitting to someone that you don't know something. Giving consideration to when and how you ask a question can make for a much smoother interaction.

So, how long should you grind away at a problem before you concede and reach out for assistance? That can be a tough call and can differ quite a bit based on your situation. Some aspects to consider are:

- *Is this meant to be a learning experience?*—If so, you'll want to spend more time looking for the answer before reaching out to anyone.

- *How long do you have to complete the task?*—The more time you have before the task is due, the more time you should spend looking for the answer yourself.

- *How busy is the rest of your team and/or your mentor?*—If no one has the time to help, you unfortunately don't have many options other than to stick it out and try to find the solution yourself until you see an opportunity to ask for help.

- *Is the sticking point something relatively "small" and holding you up from the bigger task?*—Is it something like a bug in the project setup, or a hang-up of a similar nature, that doesn't have anything directly to do with the task? These types of hang-ups can be difficult to Google, or solve by experimentation, and are scenarios where asking for help earlier than later is probably a good idea.

- *Have you worked through other aspects of the task?*—Sometimes skipping over the sticking point and working on other pieces can lead to an "aha moment." It can also help to gather multiple questions and therefore get multiple answers from one help session.

Once you've decided to reach out for help, the phrasing of the question can be important. When I ask a question, I often try to go over what I've already tried, what I've Googled, and then what exactly is stumping me. This shows that I've made a solid effort to solve it myself, gives the other person as much context as possible, and prevents the person giving assistance from experiencing the frustration of repeating the same unsuccessful troubleshooting attempts.

Most importantly, above all else, don't be afraid to ask questions. Everyone was a new developer at one point in their career, and asking questions is a legitimate way to learn.

Sincerely,

Noel

Technical decisions in the face of uncertainty

Dear new developer,

Sometimes you are confronted with decisions for which you simply don't know the correct answer. This has happened to me many times over the years.

Once, a client wanted to build an online quiz. They needed the ability to edit questions and answers without paying a developer. They wanted the quiz to feel like an application rather than a website. I had never built anything like this before, but I was the best person to choose the underlying technology.

The clock was ticking. I had to make a choice.

When you are in such a situation, you will not have time or money to do all the research you feel you need. You may be doing something that has never been done before. You may be pressed for a decision in a meeting.

If you, as a new developer, have to make a choice about a fundamental architectural decision like a platform, library, or framework, you are most likely in a small team moving fast or at a company with few engineers. You may feel in over your head and incapable of making the correct decision.

And yet, the decision still needs to be made, and you are the one who must make it. The "good-enough" decision you can make right now is better than the perfect decision that comes too late. For such important technical choices, avoid:

- Waffling on the decision
- Performing a thorough, lengthy examination of all possible solutions, putting together a spreadsheet and a set of slides to make sure you haven't missed anything
- Googling for an answer and mindlessly picking the first result
- Punting the choice to someone nontechnical
- Silently deciding without discussing the decision with team members

These will either lead to a hasty decision or a sluggish decision or waste the experience of your team.

Now you know what to avoid. What should you do instead?

First, make sure that you must make the decision. Then ensure you have the proper business context. The number of options to consider and the amount of research to be done depend on the scope of the decision.

Here are some questions to consider:

- *How much of the business will this part of the system touch?*—If it is constrained, spend less time. If you are implementing a small component or choosing a service that is only used by a portion of the organization, like GitHub for your code repository, then unwinding the choice will be easier. If you are picking a development language used for a core product, many parts of the business will depend on it, so do more research.

- *How irreversible is the decision?*—Most decisions aren't irreversible given enough time and money, but some are easier to roll back than others. Swapping out one in-memory cache provider for another is easy, but changing from one database vendor to another is more complicated. And changing a cloud provider can, depending on the amount of data involved, take years of effort.

- *Does your company have internal solutions that you might leverage?*—The bigger the company, the more likely the problem has been solved before. Finding that solution will be quicker than rebuilding it.

- *Can you defer the decision?*—Is there a manual process or a service you can buy that will solve the problem? In some cases, it is worth it even if it buys you only a few months.

Make the best decision you can with the information you have. Scale your research based on the impact on the business. However, I want to acknowledge the uncomfortable tension between knowledge and action that is at the root of any decision made with incomplete knowledge—which is to say, all of them!

This is the process I follow:

- Learn what you can. This includes finding out as much as possible about the problem, including any current solutions.

- Bounce ideas off of others in the company. Make your ideas or questions specific, both in how you ask and who you ask. This focus will help avoid analysis paralysis while still tapping others' experience.

- When you feel you have a grasp on the problem, ask for solution recommendations. Start with your current colleagues. Even if you can't find someone who has direct experience with the problem, there may be people with related know-how.

- Search the Web. See what other folks have done. If the technology is evolving, limit search results to "the past year" or you'll end up reading misleading old solutions.

- Look on social media. Find experts on social networks like Twitter and LinkedIn and ask them questions. Even better, look at their blogs and websites to see if they've already covered the topic.

- Look at communities with experienced people, such as Slacks, forums, and open source project email lists. It's better to see if your question has been answered previously rather than pop into these communities and ask right away—requests from people new to the community can annoy regular members if asked without research. But if you don't see any answers to your question, mention you searched beforehand and ask.

- Realize that no decision is perfect. In 20 years of development, I can tell you that I've never made a perfect decision—they all involved trade-offs and a lack of knowledge.

- Communicate your uncertainty to the business. This includes both concerns you have about being in over your head and any other risks that your research has found.

- Arrive at a recommendation. Get approval and buy-in from the team. Revise it based on feedback.

- Implement it.

New developer, hopefully you won't be forced to make a far-reaching architectural decision until you have more experience. But sometimes, it happens.

Oh, and if you wanted to know how my quiz conundrum ended up, some of the choices I made were implemented. Others were swapped out as the team changed and the project progressed. Overall, the app was a success.

Sincerely,

Dan

Getting answers from busy people

Dear new developer,

Busy people receive emails and requests every day. Some say email is a to-do list to which anyone can add tasks. If you want to get an answer from a busy person, you as the requester must put in effort. What that effort is depends on:

- *How big is "the ask"?*—The bigger the question you are asking, the more effort you should put in. After all, you're asking for more of their time, energy, or reputation, so the least you can do is make more effort. For example, asking for a high-level opinion on a technology is less effort than asking for help with a specific problem you are troubleshooting.

- *How well do you know the busy person?*—The less you know them, the more upfront work you should do. Contacting someone you've worked with, even years ago, is easier than a cold email to an expert you just found on LinkedIn.

- *How interested is the person in the topic you're asking about?*— If you ask me about, say, embedded C programming, you won't get a response, because, frankly, I don't know much about it. But if you asked me about software career advice for new developers, I'm likely to respond.

Effort on your part shows that you are serious. It qualifies you, especially if you persist.

However, please, don't annoy anyone. There's a line between persistence and bugging someone. My rule of thumb is to ask at most three times. Since busy people are busy, sometimes they mean to answer and the email just falls to the bottom of their inbox. I've definitely had people answer follow-up emails when I've waited a week. I always preface any email I send asking for a favor with an easy out: "hey, feel free to tell me to buzz off." And I mean it.

What does effort look like, exactly? It means asking a prepared question. It's a wash-rinse-repeat cycle of the following tasks:

- Trying to figure out your question

- Explaining your attempts in written form

- Listening to answers or suggestions

- Continuing to make progress on the question with the additional information

There's even a bonus! Struggling with the question sometimes leads you to solutions or answers without you ever contacting that busy person.

Effort shows that you are serious but doesn't guarantee an answer, unfortunately. On the other hand, putting in zero effort when communicating with a busy person usually leads to being ignored or dismissed.

Sincerely,

Dan

Ask the hard questions

Dear new developer,

In every meeting or conference call, does someone mention a concept that you don't quite understand? That often happens to me.

You hear:

- "The marketing funnel is part of the sales process."
- "We can just flurbuzz the bazznod."
- "We have plenty of runway."

That is the moment when you should ask the hard question:

- "Why is marketing connected to sales in that manner?"
- "What does that mean? I don't know what a bazznod is."
- "I'm sorry, I don't understand. Could you repeat that? How do you define runway?"

Asking these questions is important. Otherwise, everyone will be talking past each other. This will only lead to pain down the road when a misunderstanding is crystallized in people, process, or code. And you're not alone. When I have trouble understanding a concept or statement, I've found that other team members almost always do as well.

I've been asking hard questions my entire career. When I worked at a web consulting company in the early 2000s, there were often company-wide conference calls discussing our precarious financial state. I got a reputation as "the question guy" because I wasn't afraid of asking the CEO an awkward question in front of the entire company.

Here are some tips for asking hard questions:

- Pay attention before you ask. If you are asking a question which was just answered, or about something you should know, you will lack credibility.

- Don't worry about looking dumb. If it is a fuzzy concept, chances are high others in the room are unsure about the precise meaning as well.

- Ask the question from a place of humility. Make it about you. I like to use the phrase "I'm sorry, I don't understand what you just said" as a preface.

- Approach the question with positive intent. Don't ask gotcha questions or try to prove you are smarter than the speaker.

- If the answer is fuzzy or you don't understand it, consider asking a second time. "Thanks, but I'm afraid I still don't get it. Could you explain it to me again?"

- If the speaker doesn't answer or hedges again, offer to take it offline. Follow up and have the conversation later. Time may be limited and this may be the most efficient way to get your question answered.

- Recognize if the topic is sensitive—legal, personnel, or financial matters—you may not get a clear answer. At that point, getting the speaker to define terms but omit details may clarify the concept for you and is probably all you're going to get.

- Consider if anyone else in the room cares about the answer to your question. Will the audience benefit from hearing the answer? If not, then make a note to yourself to ask this later via an email, chat message, or another form of one-on-one communication.

However, consider your social capital. If you are new to the company or a new developer, you may not have much. Spend it when you must know the answer. An alternative is noting your question and asking it in a less public place—a one to one, an email, or a private chat message.

Finally, the goal here is never to "get" the speaker by asking an awkward question. Rather, it is to help get everyone on the same page.

Asking tough questions pins down nebulous concepts we work with every day. This helps everyone make better decisions.

Sincerely,

Dan

You know more than you think

Cara Borenstein is a founder at Bytebase—a collaboration tool for lightweight knowledge sharing.

Dear new developer,

A couple of years ago, I started my first job in Silicon Valley. I was a junior software engineer at a fast-moving company, and I was so excited to have the opportunity to learn. I worked hard. I looked up terms I wasn't familiar with.

I was constantly asking "how?"—"how do I do this?", "how does this work?" I was shipping code and learning fast.

Only after a number of months did I realize I was doing something wrong and letting my team down.

It came to my team's attention that we had chosen the wrong type of core technology for one of our main projects. The team leaders wanted to understand why we had chosen this technology.

I had no idea why we had chosen this technology because I had never asked. Had I asked, we would've realized pretty quickly that this technology wasn't a good choice for our system. But I was confident that my senior teammate always knew the right choices to make.

I didn't think I knew enough to ask. I had what's commonly referred to as "imposter syndrome."

My failure to ask why wasn't just a missed learning opportunity for me. It resulted in my team making an expensive mistake of choosing a wrong technology.

Now I can see that I did know enough to ask why and it was my responsibility to do so. The same goes for you, new developer.

Software engineering is a lot about trade-offs—choosing one software design over another. Design trade-offs are often not completely clear-cut, and they warrant a discussion. You don't need to have decades of experience to be able to understand the choices you and your team make. You just need to do your part to make sure your team has these discussions.

When you ask your teammates why, you push them to explain their thought processes. This helps your team to more thoroughly evaluate different options and to eventually arrive at better decisions.

Moreover, these "whys" create some of the best documentation for future engineers that join the team. If the thought process behind a choice wasn't obvious to you, it will likely be confusing to many future team members too.

How to ask "why"

Here are some tips that have worked well for me.

First, make sure that you are asking "why" with a mindset of learning and understanding, not blaming. This will shape how you phrase your question. For example, you can start your question with "I'd like to understand why we..." or "I'm unclear as to why we...".

Then identify one person who is likely best to discuss "why" with. More often than not, you'll want to start by asking one senior engineer on your team or your technical lead. After speaking with them, if there's further discussion or changes needed, you can bring this to the rest of your team together.

To initiate your question, bring it up informally without an expectation of immediately discussing it. This can be in an informal conversation, at your team's daily stand-up, or in a Slack message. For example, you might ask— "Hey teammate, I'm confused as to why we're... Do you have time later today or tomorrow to go over it?" With this approach, you can communicate your question while being respectful of your teammate's time.

How to document "why"

Now that you've asked "why," you may have driven some changes in your team's plans, but you definitely have learned something interesting. Write it down! This is some of the most useful documentation your team can have.

When writing down why, be sure to include:

- Your question
- A summary of what you discovered
- Any constraints that impacted your team's choice
- Any other options your team considered and the pros/cons
- Any action items for your team given what you learned

Ask your teammate to review your written "why" to make sure you didn't miss anything and are on the same page. Once it's approved, share it with the entire team.

If your team currently uses a wiki or shared drive solution for documentation, you can:

- Create a "start with why" folder
- Write a new document for each "why" within this folder
- Add a hypertext link to this document from each software doc that's impacted

Start asking "why"

So, new developer, asking "why" will help you learn faster and help your team make better choices. And writing down "why" will provide your team with useful documentation for future work. So get started now. Start asking "why."

Sincerely,

Cara

Trade-offs

Dear new developer,

I want to build perfect systems. There is something beautiful about flawless code solving a problem elegantly and succinctly, especially if it comes with tests and documentation.

But every time I start to work on real-world problems, trade-offs intrude. Let's take the example of a website to display information about a business. It will be updated occasionally.

Technical questions to consider when approaching this problem:

- How prominent is the business? A local coffee shop has different needs than a national retailer.
- What is the brand of the business?
- How often will updates occur?
- How many pages of information are expected?
- What is the business trying to achieve? An online presence? Acquiring future customers? Lowering customer service request frequency?
- Who will update the website? How skilled are they?
- What is the budget?
- What is the timeline?
- Who is available to do the work?

Every one of these questions influences the system I'll build. A website for a local jeweler who wants to show up in web searches, display store hours, and highlight occasional sales calls for one type of technology. A website for a regional newspaper which is to be updated hourly and handle large spikes of traffic requires a different solution.

You need to find out what the goals are and have that inform the trade-offs you make. The preceding questions will help align everyone around common objectives.

Nothing is fixed in stone, however. These choices evolve over time. I have worked on several applications that were implemented in perfectly good technologies for their time, but now feel their age.

Sincerely,

Dan

Improving Stack Overflow

Dear new developer,

Stack Overflow is the top developer question and answer site on the Internet at the time I write this. You should help improve it.

It's full of information, but there's technique in using it well. There are three different kinds of developers who use it, and you may switch between these roles:

- *Searchers*—Those who are looking for answers, usually via Google or other search engines

- *Answerers*—Those who are looking to showcase knowledge, usually by answering questions

- *Askers*—Those who have a specific question

Every developer with Internet access is a searcher. At least, I've not met any software developers who don't use Stack Overflow. But you can search haphazardly or you can search precisely.

Do it well by understanding the question you arrive at. How does it apply to your problem? Read all the answers.

Vote up both questions and answers that you find useful. Voting provides a signal to Stack Overflow and is a low effort way to add value. I know it is easier to take the first answer and move on with your current task, but please take a little time and help everyone else.

Additionally, aim to be an answerer or an asker. See if you can answer questions or add comments to clarify them. Politely point to other answers. It can be fun to improve on an existing answer too. Take the time to share your knowledge.

If you have a question and you find that it hasn't been answered on Stack Overflow, take time to build out a solid question post. If you end up finding the answer to your query, self-answer it to help future searchers.

Any help you provide on Stack Overflow will last for years and will touch many. Currently, I have approximately 4000 reputation points on Stack Overflow, but my questions and answers have reached over a million people.

Sincerely,

Dan

How to say "I don't know"

Dear new developer,

When you are asked a question that you can't answer, but you kinda, sorta might be able to come up with a plausible response, it is tempting to just wing it. Few people enjoy admitting ignorance. I know I do not.

One word of advice for you: *Don't.*

Why not just guess? Your guess may have negative consequences. Let's cover a few possibilities:

- Your answer could be incorrect and be revealed as such by another team member immediately. In this case, you have egg on your face because you were wrong. People may forgive this once or twice, but in time trust in you will erode.

- Your suggestion could be incorrect and not be discovered until later, perhaps by a user reporting a bug or through data loss. This negatively affects the system.

- You could be correct, but for the wrong reasons. You will probably suggest this answer in the future. But since you don't really know why this answer is correct, you won't know when it's not applicable.

I hope I've convinced you that it's a bad idea to guess. What to do instead? The right way to answer is to say: "I don't know but let me find out." Let's break that down.

First, you admit that you aren't certain of the answer. But you then focus on what the questioner really wants: a correct answer. That's what you're promising them.

Next, write down the question. A notepad, your calendar, email it to yourself—any way you won't forget it. Carve out some time to find the right answer.

Finally, follow up. If it's a weighty or thorny question, provide status updates as you make progress. Feel free to collaborate with your team and the questioner as well—you own finding the answer, but that doesn't mean you can't ask for help.

By the way, if you believe what you said is correct, but are wrong, that's a different type of error—one that I find more forgivable. Technology changes all the time. If, for instance, you "knew" that it was appropriate to concatenate your web assets to minimize browser connect requests to improve your website performance, you'd be correct in a world of HTTP/1.1. But in a world of HTTP/2, concatenating assets has little to no benefit.

Internet protocols aside, the point is it's okay to be wrong.

But when someone asks you a question and you aren't sure of the answer, don't just guess. Say "I don't know," then find out.

Sincerely,

Dan

In conclusion

Asking questions, in the right way and at the right time, helps you find the knowledge you need to do your job. You can ask questions in person. You can ask them of the crowds on the Internet. You can even ask them of yourself.

Be prepared. Do the research. And when you have to make a decision based on less than perfect information, scale your efforts based on the impact of the choice.

Writing

Writing is an art form. Conveying meaning clearly without feedback from your audience is hard. However, for a software engineer, writing clear prose is often the best way to communicate. Writing is:

- *Asynchronous*—You can write a question at 8 a.m. and someone can read it and give you an answer at 5 p.m.

- *Shareable*—If knowledge is written, you can share it with others easily.

- *Clarifying*—Whether I am documenting for others or for myself, it's easy for me to say or think something vague or unclear. But when I write it down, the uncertainty or doublethink is easier to detect.

- *Durable*—When you write, the resulting document can exist for years, if not decades. When someone else needs to understand what you learned, they can get an answer even if you are not available.

Of course, writing isn't just for sharing knowledge. It's also for discussion, explanation, and connection. Writing is an underappreciated engineering skill, and you'll be a better developer for practicing it.

© Dan Moore 2020
D. Moore, *Letters to a New Developer*, https://doi.org/10.1007/978-1-4842-6074-6_3

Read your work aloud

Dear new developer,

One of the best ways to improve your writing is to read it. Doing so will help you edit and refine your text. But speaking the words aloud helps more than a silent reread.

For some reason, when I am silently reading something I've written, I skip over awkward phrases or misplaced words. This is especially true if I've been working on a document for a while.

But reading the words aloud doesn't just help with typos and awkwardness. It will also help you notice the cadence and word choice. Are there run-on sentences, with three or four clauses strung together? Do! You! Overuse! Exclamation points? Have you used the same word three times in the last paragraph? Do you use jargon or acronyms when simpler terms would suffice?

I find all these flaws easier to gloss over when I am reading a document silently. Don't trust me? Read this next sentence silently and then aloud:

This a is a simple sentence.

When I scan that sentence, I skip over the typo. Did you? I notice it when I read the sentence aloud. Speaking written text forces you to slow down. In my experience, the denser and more complex the concepts in my writing, the easier it is to skip over errors and awkwardness when reading it silently.

I read my work out loud whenever I can, before submitting a post or sending an email, because the process improves the end product. I have spoken every word on every page of this book.

It does take longer, so I sometimes don't have time; I also won't do it with quick emails—I don't read "yes, that works" out loud when replying to a scheduling request. But many emails and chat messages benefit from being read aloud, and all longer-lived documentation does as well.

Give it a try.

Sincerely,

Dan

Write that down!

John Obelenus solves problems and saves time through software and crushing entropy.

Dear new developer,

Even when I was a kid in school, I hardly wrote things down. That's why we had textbooks after all! I was baffled by other students in college furiously transcribing every word that came out of the professor's mouth. Now I have a career in the world of software where we track everything. Git holds all the code commits, email is never really deleted, and project management and issue tracking tools keep track of what we're doing and have done. How could anything go missing?

I am constantly looking for things and cannot find them. I get a bug report, look at the code, and say to myself, "That is obviously wrong, let's fix it." I look at the offending commit that introduced the bug (of course, it was me). But what is not there? The reason for the change. So I look at the project management tool we use. And someone definitely asked for a change, but I'm still not sure why. So I search through my email for the few days before I made the change, and…nothing. I still can't really figure out why we all decided to make a change which introduced a bug.

Or, worse yet, someone asks for a change. All well and good. Then a month later, someone asks to change it back. You shake your head and make the change. Then someone is confused why this is happening and calls a meeting and invites you to help figure it out. What are you going to bring to this meeting? Did you write anything down? I never used to. Now I do.

Now I have a notepad next to my laptop. And I have a notebook on the shelf. I make better use of git messages and write down who asked for changes. When working on a feature, or a bug, and I finding something "interesting," I make a GitHub wiki entry explaining it. I write a comment in the codebase explaining it. There are two kinds of documentation—useful documentation and redundant documentation.

No doubt many people have told you to comment your code. I hope many people have told you never to comment a loop with `// loop over the array`. That is not increasing clarity, it is just duplicating what the code is doing— adding noise, not signal. My contention is that comments are rarely useful for explaining "What this code does…" but are far more useful when explaining "Because of X, we are going to do…."

The future you is going to be very happy if you start documenting the intent behind what you're doing. Good code is easy to read. Bad code is capable of being understood with time. But code doesn't tell you why you're doing all this work in the first place. Maybe something has changed and you don't even need this code anymore—deleting code is the most satisfying feeling. But you won't know unless you know the intent, the purpose, of the code. And the rest of the folks you're working with are going to be very happy as well.

If you write everything down (and make it public), they won't need to tap you on the shoulder when you're in "the zone" to ask. When someone wants to set a meeting to understand why things are "the way they are," you will have already captured that information. You can send them the link and kill the meeting (okay, maybe killing meetings is more satisfying than killing code).

We only have so much time in our life, and we already work long hours. Let's make future us happier by writing things down, so we don't have to figure it all out again. We figured it out once when we wrote the code. Capture the knowledge in that moment in time. And write it down!

Sincerely,

John Obelenus

Tips for using email well

Dear new developer,

For all the hullabaloo about chat systems like Slack and Microsoft Teams, email still rules the roost when it comes to cross-organization communication. It is the baseline across every business I've worked in.

Everyone has an email address. Email communication is auditable. And it's immutable after it has been sent, to the chagrin of anyone who has ever hit send and wished immediately they could call the message back. If you want to communicate with a vendor or candidate, you don't have to get them access to your chat system. To send an email to anyone in the world, you only need to know the recipient's email address.

Email is often an organization's permanent record of documentation and decisions. Chat systems also try to provide this, but email is prevalent. I remember one founder had a Gmail account that dated back to the start of the company. He would sometimes pull up and forward email chains from years back as they became relevant again.

Email is great at conveying information, but awful at conveying context. A poorly written email can be puzzling. Because email is asynchronous, this can cause slowdowns and confusion, whereas the same lack of clarity in a real-time conversation is addressed in the moment. For example, when someone uses the word "tomorrow" and today is Friday, you can ask "when you said tomorrow, do you mean Saturday or Monday, the next business day?"

The clarity and tone with which you write your email influences how you are perceived in your company. How can you make your email communication more effective?

- Keep an email as short as possible. Many people are reading or responding to email on their phone, and overly long emails can be unpleasant.

- If your email must be long, add an executive summary at the top. If you are asking for a decision, make that clear and then provide the context further below. It doesn't have to be fancy: "I think we should upgrade our PostgreSQL database. What's your opinion? More details below." works great.

- If it is a sensitive topic, are you sure you want to use email? Consider a face-to-face or other high bandwidth conversations instead and then write up an email to capture the context and any decisions made. If the other party has a differing understanding, get back into the meeting room, on the phone, or into a video call.

- Email chains are hard to follow. Add links to supporting documents rather than attaching them. Consider taking the content from a long email and putting it into a document.

- Avoid using relative time references. Because email is asynchronous, you never know when your email will be read. An example of a poor time reference: "We're upgrading our PostgreSQL database tomorrow." When exactly is "tomorrow"? "We're upgrading our PostgreSQL database on Thur Mar 26" is far better. Bonus points for adding the timezone: "We're upgrading our PostgreSQL database on Thur Mar 26 at 5pm Mountain Standard Time" has no ambiguity at all.

- Keep your emails focused. A laundry list of questions or issues is fine, as long as they all relate. Email threads which change topics over time lead to confusion. You aren't paying by the subject line, so use a new one.

Email is a powerful mode of communication. Make sure you use it well.

Sincerely,

Dan

Real-time messaging

Dear new developer,

Chat systems, like Slack and Microsoft Teams, are common ways for developers to communicate. These real-time messaging systems are asynchronous but can be conversational if both parties are present. You can cut and paste with ease, making them a great way to share technical troubleshooting information. They provide a written record of discussions with timestamps. And they can be integrated with other systems like monitoring and alerting to provide historical context for actions.

But while this is a written medium, it has different characteristics than email or long form writing. Here are some tips about how to use chat systems:

- *Default to public*—One of the benefits of using chat is that it is searchable. If you ask a question about a system component, later on someone can search for it. They'll either find the answer or see that the question wasn't answered, also a signal. But if you aren't having chats in public channels, the future searcher can't find it. It can be scary to put your ignorance out there with a public query, but it is better for the organization in the long term to default to public communication.

- *Use higher bandwidth options for sensitive conversations*— Chat is flat. Even with gifs and emojis, it doesn't have the emotional depth of a phone call. If you want to discuss something fraught with feeling, do it in person, over a video call, or using the phone, in that order. Performance discussions, for example, can lead to misunderstandings and hurt if conducted over chat. If a conversation appears to be heading toward sensitive topics, it's okay to say "hey, can we go to video?"

- *Consider other forms of communication when chat runs long*—Much the same as the previous point, if you are troubleshooting a technical issue, it's often much quicker to hop on a screen share or walk over and talk in person. Don't be afraid to use chat to start a conversation but finish it in other ways.

- *Follow up with chat*—Summing up a discussion with a chat has the same benefits as a summary email. Such a chat review makes sure everyone agrees what was decided and records it for future reference.

- *Set boundaries*—Responding to chats feels like accomplishing real work. And it is, as communication is a key part of software development. But set your boundaries and communicate them. I turn off notifications as soon as I install Slack because I want to view the messages on my schedule, not whenever I get a "ding." I also don't install Slack on my phone because in the past I've checked my work Slack messages after hours, which didn't feel great. Discuss appropriate boundaries around chat communication with your team.

Slack and other chat systems have unique benefits, but their intrusive communication methods and lack of context mean that you can't treat them as equivalent to other forms of written communication.

Sincerely,

Dan

Write a technical ebook

Dear new developer,

I suggest you take some free time and write a technical ebook. Doing so will give you a deep understanding of what you write about. It will also give you credibility. You can use the writing process to make connections and give talks at meetups. An ebook may even make you some money—but don't count on that.

Pick a technology that you use at work or on a side project. You should look for a technology with the following attributes:

- Only a few books have been written about it.

- You are interested in the subject and want to deeply learn it.

- You use it regularly.

- The technology is either new and dynamic, like React, and you're excited to keep the book up to date, or it is old and static, like bash.

- It is relatively popular.

Please, learn from my mistakes. When I wrote a 40-page ebook about a command-line tool for Cordova,[1] a framework for writing mobile applications, I made a few errors:

- The market for Cordova books was small, and the subset of people interested in automation of Cordova projects was even smaller.

- I picked the technology because my employer was using it, but after one project, we stopped. I wasn't really interested in mobile development so I never updated the book. That meant it quickly became out of date.

Topics that aren't about a particular technology have a longer shelf life. How to manage a software team has changed some in the last 20 years, but how to build a large-scale JavaScript application has changed in the last 12 months.

When you select a topic, don't jump right into drafting the book. Instead, outline it and write sections of the book over time. An easy way to do this is to create a category on your blog (you do have a blog, right?) and post regularly about it.

Writing the book in sections is low risk. If you write two posts about the technology and you are bored out of your mind, stop. After four or five posts, you'll know this is a topic to which you want to commit. Now, start looking for communities where the technology is discussed. Answer questions and respond to discussions. If a question is especially interesting or brought up frequently, write a post to answer it and share that. Set up an email list on your blog to capture visitors who want to be kept up to date with your posts. You can then market to this engaged audience when your book is published.

Once you have about 20 posts, start pulling them together to form an ebook. After you start writing the ebook, include a link to your book site in the signature of any community posting you do to help market the book. I used Leanpub[2] and had a great experience—you get a free book website, and they handle payments and publishing in various formats. With this choice, you are responsible for not just writing the book, but marketing it. However, you get to keep the lion's share of the revenue.

You can also contact a publisher and see if they'd be interested in your book. They'll take more of each dollar of revenue, but will provide editing, marketing, and other services. They also have credibility with readers. For a niche book like the one I wrote, the market was so small that I don't think a publisher would have been interested. Of course, that might have been good information for me to know, too.

---

[1]https://cordova.apache.org/
[2]https://leanpub.com/

I made about $700 from my ebook. I don't think I ever calculated the exact hourly rate, but I can say with confidence that it was far lower than I could have made writing code.

So, why is writing an ebook a valuable use of your time?

Not for the money.

For the glory? Perhaps. It's possible your book will open some doors.

But really, I recommend it because the ability to persist in creating a large, complex product based on research and understanding is a foundational aspect of successful software product delivery. In other words, writing an ebook and launching a software system are similar. Writing a book also challenges you to think deeply and broadly. You must think deeply to understand the technology and write about it in a way other people can understand. And you must think broadly to create a cohesive whole. This is similar to holding a complex software system in your mind.

Sincerely,

Dan

On developer documentation

Dear new developer,

I love documentation. I like writing it, and when it's well written, I love reading it. There are many types of documentation, and they aren't all the same. Some illustrate what you can do with a consumer product. Some nail down exactly what will be accomplished between two business parties. But what I'm writing about in this letter is software documentation for developers.

Good documentation of this type cuts down on communication between software engineers, increasing team scalability. At a former company, each developer had a copy of the application server to develop against. Every time a new developer rolled on to the project, this environment had to be set up. Either the new developer had to do it, or someone else did.

I was involved in setting up the first one or two instances, but I got tired of that task quickly. I wrote a step-by-step onboarding document which enabled incoming developers to do the setup themselves. This was good for me, as it saved me time, good for the new team member as it gave them a greater understanding of the platform on which they were developing, and good for the project, as if I got hit by a bus, the knowledge of how to set up a development environment wasn't lost.

Documentation has come to my rescue more than once. It often captures information that I or others struggled to find. We may need this information but use it infrequently. For example, I once imported a project I was working on into Eclipse, a Java IDE. It wasn't a cakewalk. I wrote down how I did this, but a few months later, I couldn't have told you the first thing about it. That knowledge had been evicted from my brain. But, should I have a need to do another import, I can! The knowledge is stored safely in text.

Comments in code can also be a developer documentation. When writing these, focus on the why behind a decision, not the nuts and bolts. Which is better?

- ```
  // We convert from Central timezone to UTC here,
  using the standard library.
  ```

- ```
  // This module exists because we had to integrate
  with the Acme data feed. They store timestamps
  in the Central timezone, which is why we do the
  conversion here.
  ```

I'll take the second comment all day long, thanks. It gives me context, and I can ask teammates about the Acme data feed if I need more. Names of classes, functions, and variables are great ways to document intent as well, and these have the virtue of being harder to neglect. Yes, you can change the logic without changing the name of a method, but developers are more likely to modify that name than they are to update the comments, in my experience.

Documentation is a great way to get started in open source as well. Many projects have working code, but minimal docs. But such documentation is important in helping engineers unfamiliar with the project get started. Look in the issue tracker of your favorite open source project and see if any documentation needs to be written or updated. Even fixing a typo or clarifying a confusing sentence makes the project better. It's a great way to "give back" to open source projects you are passionate about.

There are two objections to developer focused documentation that I'd like to address.

One is that it quickly becomes outdated. This is true. It takes effort to maintain documentation. When I change a process or system attribute that requires updating docs, I remind myself of the benefits mentioned earlier. If I can convince myself that I will save more time in the long run by documenting because I won't have to explain the changes to others or myself, then I do it. I'm not always successful, I'll admit.

Out-of-date documentation can be very frustrating. You can either remove the documentation or loudly mark it "OUT OF DATE" if it will illuminate past decisions. Either way, help people avoid archaic developer documentation.

The other issue is what I call the "protecting your job" excuse for avoiding documentation. If you don't document what you've done, you have a secure job—especially if it's an important piece of the system. But that job security is a chain that binds. In addition to indicating distrust of your team or management, it also means when a different, better, internal opportunity comes along, you won't be able to take it. Since no one else knows how to do your job, you're stuck.

Not exactly good for your personal growth, eh? And that is the best-case scenario. It assumes that your team won't work around you and devalue the code that you're "protecting."

Well-written developer documentation scales your knowledge across your team, organization, or the world.

Sincerely,

Dan

Always be journaling

Brooke Kuhlmann has been developing software for ~20 years with an emphasis in the Ruby and Elm languages. He runs Alchemists, a collective devoted to the craft, quality, ethics, and security of software engineering.

Dear new developer,

Of the many techniques you'll pick up over the course of your career, one worth investing in early is journaling. Journaling might not seem like a worthy endeavor at first. Capturing important moments of your life every day might seem like extra work on top of everything else you are juggling in your life but, in time, journaling will pay dividends if you stay disciplined and detailed. As you grow older, the details of earlier experiences will grow foggy in your mind. Being able to reconstitute past experiences in order to apply them to present situations will help you make more informed decisions.

Additionally, journaling serves another purpose; it makes you a better writer. This is a wonderful skill to have which shouldn't be underestimated. In addition to technical expertise, being able to express your thoughts succinctly, supported with documented details, is a sought-after skill. Exercising this part of your mind on a regular basis will allow you to keep this skill sharp.

Organization

How you organize your journal entries is up to you. Everyone is different, and there is no right or wrong way to do this as long as it makes sense, is easy to add new entries, and can be searched through quickly. To start with, journal entries are meant to be chronological, so it does help to use a date/time structure, for example:

Format: <year>/<month>/<day>/<hour>/<minute>/<second>

Example: 2018/12/01/10/10/10

The use of categories (for high-level organization) and tags (for associations across categories) can be helpful too. Useful categories to start with could include:

- *Work*—Lessons learned from paid work. In addition to the benefits of helping you stay organized and not letting important ideas slip through the cracks, this also serves as a way to measure the pulse on how you are feeling about the work you are doing and the progress being made. When you look back over time and see a rocky or downward curve, it might be time to move on to something new. On the other hand, the use of your journal might be motivational, can serve as a reminder to explore previous ideas in greater detail, and can even help solve current problems.

- *Side projects*—Lessons you want to capture related to open source software, hobbies, and so on that might be worth sharing in a public forum at some point but currently are raw material.

- *Personal*—For private thoughts and ideas of use only to you. This might include your health, mood, personal reflections, or relationships.

For tags, you might want to use a single tag or multiple tags in order to break down journal entries beyond high-level categories. Tags make it easier to search for entries faster when, for example, you have a dotfiles project you've been working on and you have it tagged as "dotfiles." Using multiple tags helps connect related journal entries across categories which is another nice way to group information.

It never hurts to have a few tools to ease this organization of your thoughts. Here are some recommendations:

- *Bear*—Supports macOS, iOS, and watchOS. Has great sync capability between desktop and mobile, hybrid Markdown support, and tends to be a more free form in that you can organize and tag information however you see fit. It's free to get started and $15/year to add pro and sync features.

- *Day One*—Supports macOS, iOS, and watchOS. Tends to be more specialized for journaling but isn't always the easiest to manage. It's free to get started but $35/year for pro features.

- *Notes*—Native to macOS and iOS, provides a free solution for getting started with sync capabilities.

Schedule

Choose a schedule for writing journal entries that you are comfortable with. I would recommend, at a minimum, to journal daily, even if briefly. It's up to you to be disciplined about this as only you will benefit. You can schedule this as a recurring action in your task manager or as a calendar event. Use whatever best fits your workflow and be diligent about it.

In addition to scheduling, you can capture important events as they occur such as thoughts while in a meeting or when working on complex technical issues. Yes, a journal can also be a helpful scratch pad for further reflective and refined thought later. If real-time journaling isn't enough, try scheduling an end-of-day reminder to reflect on the day's experiences.

Automation is key to being successful so figure out what works best for your mind and mode of operation. Here are some scheduling tools worth adding to your toolbox:

- *OmniFocus*—Based on David Allen's *Getting Things Done* book. It can cost over $100 when you buy the macOS and iOS versions, but syncing is free. It's a powerful tool and worth the investment.

- *Fantastical*—If task managers are not for you, consider investing in good calendar software and set up recurring events/reminders that way.

- *Reminders*—Doesn't have a lot of bells and whistles but will help get you started until you outgrow it. Free for macOS and iOS.

Reviews

In order to learn from past mistakes and experiences and build upon earlier lessons, it is important to review and reflect on your progress. A good rule of thumb is to conduct this kind of "self-retrospective" weekly, monthly, and yearly.

This'll help keep where you have been and where you are headed in perspective. Plus, it's nice to see how far you've come or gone off the tracks in case you need to pivot or course correct.

Personal results

Over the years, maintaining a journal has made me:

- *A stronger writer*—As mentioned earlier, since I've been journaling, I've found I've become much stronger when writing git commits, responding to group chat responses, creating pull requests, replying to emails, and so on. I find my content is structured and well composed rather than short, terse, or staccato.

- *A stronger learner*—When capturing and reflecting on the various experiences of your past life, you can see connections that weren't there before. It's fascinating when I reflect on past work and realize I've forgotten a tool or technique that I didn't fully understand at the time. Now I have much more knowledge and context for how to apply that to the current situation and thus have saved myself additional time.

- *A stronger mentor*—When you accumulate a lot of experience and expertise, you can forget the source of your tacit knowledge. I've found being able to search for and share recorded knowledge so others may learn and grow in a similar manner helps make you a fount of information.

Closing thoughts

Your future self will thank your past self for recording this history. Being able to understand the long tail of your work—and therefore your life—is valuable in making informed decisions on what actions you'll take next. Mine this information often because your experiences are gold.

Sincerely,

Brooke

You should blog

Dear new developer,

A blog is free, forces you to think, provides an example of your ability to explain concepts, and helps others.

What's not to like?

The hardest part about blogging is doing it. Now, I am no Fred Wilson,[3] who blogged every day for 15+ years, but I have blogged since 2003. I've written at least once every month of those years, except one—I must have been super busy in November 2011.

From personal experience, I can tell you that blogging probably won't get you a job, but it can lead to contracts. It won't make you a superstar but will provide credibility. It won't make you an excellent writer, but it will improve your ability to convey your thoughts.

What should you write about?

This is one of the questions I am asked whenever I suggest starting a blog. There are many possible answers: the latest problem you faced at work, the technology that interests you, or simply excerpt and comment on an interesting story.

Blogging reflects an ongoing curiosity about software development or whatever topic you choose. When you commit to writing one, you're not searching for a broad audience. But a regular blog will attract those with like-minded interests.

It doesn't really matter what the topic is as long as you are interested in writing about it. Technology changes fast enough and is broad enough that you'll always have something to write about. For example, if you are passionate about JavaScript, possible topics include how you set up your JavaScript coding environment, a new keyword you learned, the difference between === and ==, or the way you debugged a troublesome issue. You are writing to learn, for the clarity prose brings, and to share your knowledge with the world.

Don't reveal any trade secrets of your employer, however. If you have any inkling that what you are writing about might be sensitive, run your desire to blog by your manager.

One more thing: You must commit. Six months is a good minimum.

The commitment matters. The benefits of blogging don't accrue on the first or second post, but on the twenty-first or twenty-second. Search engines start to notice your blog after a couple of months. You can review your posts and see patterns. Someone who you don't even know will read a post and find it useful—it is inspiring when a stranger emails you out of the blue and thanks you for what you've written.

So, how do you start?

I was at a conference once. During a question and answer session, I was asked about how to start blogging. I started to spout off about using WordPress, and the questioner clarified: "What about Medium?"

---

[3]He blogs at https://avc.com

I stopped short. The correct answer was actually "whatever is easiest." The technology is immaterial, especially when you are starting. Here are some tips on what actually matters.

Realize that almost no one will read your blog, especially in the beginning. Now, why would you write if no one will read it? To clarify your thoughts, to provide yourself a written record, and because, if you keep at it, Google and other search engines will find it.

Search engines are great at exposing the long tail of the Internet. If you write interesting posts, eventually Google will find it, and real live people will follow.

Here are some numbers to illustrate. I started a blog in 2018. Table 3-1 shows the number of posts and visits for each month.

Table 3-1. First six months of visitors and posts for the Letters to a New Developer blog

Month	Posts	Visitors
September 2018	8	5
October 2018	11	20
November 2018	6	15
December 2018	9	219
January 2019	8	221
February 2019	9	223

For the first month, I wrote more posts than I had visitors! For the first three months, I wrote 25 posts and had 40 visitors. If you aren't ready and willing to commit for six months, your blog will be one of those slightly sad blogs with three interesting posts, then one post six months later with the title "I haven't posted in a while..." and then silence.

Now, if occasional posting is what you desire, that's fine—there are many different reasons to blog. But if you are looking to be read by others, an abandoned blog won't help.

As I mentioned earlier, commit to writing your blog for at least six months. Some techniques I used to commit when I started that blog in 2018:

- I wrote out 10–20 exciting blog post titles. If I couldn't come up with that many ideas, I was not passionate enough about the topic. That's okay. Better to find out before investing the effort of writing one or two of them.

- I emailed myself whenever I had a blog post idea. This let me search my email when I had time to write but no ideas. You can capture ideas with a spreadsheet, doc, Trello board, or to-do list. Just make sure you capture the inspiration when it strikes.

- I made occasional posts easier by excerpting interesting articles or writing a response to ideas presented in other blogs or articles.

- I wrote blog posts ahead of time and scheduled them to post weekly. When the muse is present, it feels easy to write a few posts. When the muse is absent, prescheduling let me take a break while still displaying consistency.

- I realized and accepted that some of my posts were average or even mediocre. It is embarrassing to put out crappy content. Don't do that. But some posts are better than others. Volume is key, and the longer you blog, the better your typical post will get.

As far as blogging software, the topic of that question asked at the conference I mentioned above? Use whatever is comfortable and easy. That may be WordPress.com, Medium, or Hugo/Middleman/Jekyll/the latest shiny static site generation framework.

Whatever you choose, don't let the technology impede the writing. As a developer, it can be more fun to be in the weeds tweaking your blog deployment pipeline or page compilation than it is to write a post. At least it has been that way for me. But focusing on the tooling will distract you from your goal, which is to write.

My final tip is to share your posts in online communities. This creates links and traffic. It will also put your content in front of knowledgeable people who will poke holes in your logic and challenge your ideas. This process hurts sometimes, but feedback will make your writing better.

Which community should you share your posts with? Find where your people are. There are many online communities, whether tech specific like Hacker News, general purpose like Twitter, or focused and private like a DevOps Slack. Sharing is how I was able to increase the number of visitors to my blog in December 2018.

It doesn't matter which community you choose, as long as you are an active member and sharing an on-topic post. However, don't share only your own work; that's self-promotion, not community participation. Find other interesting links, add comments, or answer questions. I find community members are skeptical of newcomers who join, drop their own links, and leave. I have received scoldings when I posted links that I thought were interesting but were not in line with the community's values or tastes. It stung, but I accepted the judgment, acknowledged my mistake, and did better afterward.

Blogging requires a plan. It's a great way to amplify your voice, display your expertise, and share your knowledge. Commit to it and set yourself up for success.

Sincerely,

Dan

Motivation

Dear new developer,

Writing is hard. It can be tough to keep going. Here are some reasons why I've written for more than 15 years and why I'll do so for the foreseeable future:

- *Writing crystallizes my thoughts*—Writing, especially a deep technical piece, clarifies my understanding of the problem. If it is public, it is like writing an email to the world. Sometimes my writing process turns up issues or concepts not previously considered or other questions to research. It's easy to hold a fuzzy concept in my mind, but when written down, the holes in my ideas are evident.

- *Writing builds my credibility*—I have made money because people found my blog. I've had people interview me for positions and mention it. It's easy to say "I know technology ABC" in an interview or consulting discussion, but it is more powerful to say "Ah yes, I've seen technology ABC before. I wrote a post about it, let me send that to you."

- *Writing helps others*—Friends looking for help with a technology or tool sometimes mention they found my blog while searching. Given the size of the Internet, this warms my heart. I've searched myself and stumbled onto a post of mine. The post solved my problem, so I was appreciative of my past self for taking the time to write it. I have been helped tremendously by others' docs, so I consider writing "paying it forward."

I write in public far more often than I write in private. But writing I share with no one has helped me think about problems I had or issues I faced as well. I don't often review what I wrote, but the act of writing forced me to confront my thoughts.

Writing in public for years, on the other hand, has helped shape my career. It's a historical record both prospective employers and I can review. It illustrates my ability to convey technical information and context.

Once an interviewer confessed to reviewing my blog. We had a discussion around the technical details of one of my posts. I got that contract.

Sincerely,

Dan

In conclusion

For software engineers, writing understandable prose is invaluable. The systems we build can be immensely complex, long-lived, and maintained by many people. This means that we must document them. Humans have found no better way than text to densely convey information over long timeframes.

But writing is also good for knowledge with a shorter life span. Whether that is a quick question on a chat system, a blog post, or a note to yourself, the act of writing forces clarity in a way that speech or thoughts do not.

As developers, we often focus on programming and technical skills. Writing well is often dismissed as a "soft skill." But communicating ideas is something that both code and writing do, each in their own way. Practice your writing, focus your thoughts, and hone your ability to communicate.

In Conclusion

Tools to Learn

As software developers, we stand on the shoulders of giants. Software engineers are both toolmakers and tool consumers. Amazingly, many of these useful tools are freely distributed and free to use.

Tools like text editors, version control, and automated tests are used every day in the development and operation of systems. Knowing the syntax of your programming language isn't enough. You should learn these widely used tools too.

Leverage

Dear new developer,

You need to deliver more with less. Leverage makes you more productive, able to build and deliver better solutions in less time. Tools offer leverage. They also make the job more fun. It is a joy to write software, but for me the true delight of development is building solutions to help people. Tools accelerate development, increase stability, and provide additional functionality beyond what a team can build in a given timeline and budget.

Here are some tools to increase your software delivery capacity:

- *A test suite*—A suite provides leverage by serving as living documentation and allowing others to understand the code. It also guarantees that fixed bugs remain fixed so that changes to the system can be made without affecting software that depends on it. This lets you fearlessly evolve the system and incorporate new libraries, algorithms, or techniques.

© Dan Moore 2020
D. Moore, *Letters to a New Developer*, https://doi.org/10.1007/978-1-4842-6074-6_4

- *Libraries and frameworks, such as Ruby on Rails*—By solving common problems, libraries let you build software faster. Because of their wide usage, they handle edge cases that your users would find if you built your own solution.

- *IaaS (infrastructure as a service) offerings, like AWS EC2*— These services provide servers and other infrastructure which you can use APIs (application programming interfaces) to manage. You can apply software engineering techniques to the environment in which your code runs. This lets you ensure consistency of your infrastructure and make deployments repeatable.

- *PaaS (platform as a service) solutions, like Heroku*—These offerings constrain your application's architecture, but remove a whole host of operations tasks and choices from your plate, such as deployment tooling and patching servers. When a bug affects a web server, you don't spend time checking each of your servers—the provider does. This allows you to focus on business logic.

- *SaaS (software as a service) solutions, like Google Apps*— These are an entire snap-in service for a fee, rather than a service you write custom code to use, like IaaS and PaaS solutions. These vary in size and scope, but may integrate with your software.

Leverage makes you more productive. Seek it.

Sincerely,

Dan

The command line

Dear new developer,

I remember the first time I saw a senior engineer struggle with the command line. He had just rolled onto a client project. If memory serves, he was trying to set up his IDE for a Java application.

I noticed him with the command-line window open, trying to navigate around source code directories. I wondered why he was having difficulty. I felt the same way some developers probably feel about me when I struggle with CSS or cutting up a PDF or reading C—"how are you a developer without understanding this?" It cemented in my mind why a new developer should learn the command line inside and out.

It's a baseline.

The command-line interface (also known as the CLI) will always be available—wherever you are (unless you are on an old Mac, pre-Mac OS X, in which case, *why?*). This is in contrast to the graphical user interface (GUI) which is omnipresent on desktop machines but missing from many other software environments.

Unlike the other skills I mentioned earlier, knowing how to navigate the command line will make your developer experience better no matter where you work. It's a general-purpose skill, like understanding how to use version control or learning a text editor.

Let's take a simple task—I need to move a file into a directory, change the permissions on that file, then look through the file for a certain phrase: "rosebud." With a CLI, I can:

- *Accomplish the task in less time*—I can move files, change permissions, and search the files far faster with CLI tools than I can with any GUI tools. The first few times I try this, I will be slower on the command line than if I were using a GUI. You must learn the CLI and the cues to help you do so are minimal. You also must learn a GUI, but there are more hints—this is why most computers nowadays have GUIs. But once I know the CLI commands, typing will be much quicker than moving the mouse through the GUI.

- *Redo or repeat the tasks*—If I'm trying to do this sample task, I can do this one time in the GUI easily, using the mouse and menu commands. But repeating this task, whether once a day, once a month, or on every software release, becomes tedious and error prone. On the other hand, I can do it once in the CLI and then take the CLI commands and put them into a script. A script is a text file with commands that can run them one after the other. The same commands will be run every time I execute the script. My example is simple, but if the task is complex, getting it right once and having a script will save time and energy. All the commands in the script will run in exactly the same way every time. If you don't do the task often, you will save time with a script because you won't have to reconstruct the exact commands executed.

- *Easily share the task script with others*—If others want to perform this task, using a GUI you could record a video of yourself clicking around. Or you could write down each step in detail and share the document. If you are physically collocated, you could walk over and show someone how to do it. With a CLI, it's much easier. You send someone an executable script they can run. If they have access to the same command-line programs and data, they'll get the same results. However, the same command-line program can have different versions, so beware of that possibility.

Hopefully, I've convinced you of the benefits of the command line. Now, what are good ways to learn it?

I think that one path is to jump in. Find the "terminal" program if you use a Mac or the "cmd" program if you use Windows. Open it up. Search on the Web for "command-line tutorial <your platform here>" and work through a tutorial. I personally learn best when I have a real task. If you do too, think of a task you do frequently: opening up a number of files for a project or copying files to a backup directory. Do it once in the GUI. Then do it once in the CLI. Then make a script for it. See how that process feels. If you worry about destroying your computer, use a temporary directory and fake files.

Another option is to map between a GUI program such as your code editor and the CLI. Every time you do a task in the GUI, drop down into the CLI and repeat it. For many programs, if it can be done in the GUI, it can be done in the CLI. CLI-compatible tasks can be as simple as renaming a file and as complex as a many step process to build multiple programs.

As you become more comfortable, you may have the option of sharing your keybindings between your editor and your shell. A keybinding is a fancy way to say assigning commands to various keys on your keyboard. Search for "keybindings <editor> <shell>". I use vi keybindings for my bash shell, and it lets me easily move around the CLI. And every time I learn a new way to move around the editor, my CLI experience improves.

The command line is present on every modern computer. Learning it will save you time, allow you to automate common actions, and let you share those solutions. Well worth the effort.

Sincerely,

Dan

jq, awk, and sed

Dear new developer,

You will work with text files containing structured data at some point in your development career. These are stored in many different formats, including tab-separated variables (TSV), comma-separated variables (CSV), or JavaScript

Object Notation (JSON). You may want to extract data, ingest information, or examine log entries. You may be transforming data from one format to another.

If this happens frequently, you should write a tool to help you. Sometimes, though, processing these files is a one-off, and writing a full-fledged tool is overkill. An alternative is to learn some of the Unix tools. Here are three that I consider "table stakes" for a developer. In Listing 4-1, you can see sample lines from a web server log. We'll process these lines in a few different ways.

Listing 4-1. *Web server access log lines, stored in a file named logs.txt*

```
54.147.20.92 - - [26/Jul/2019:20:21:04 -0600] "GET /wordpress HTTP/1.1" 301
241 "-" "Slackbot 1.0 (+https://api.slack.com/robots)"
185.24.234.106 - - [26/Jul/2019:20:20:50 -0600] "GET /wordpress/archives/
date/2004/02 HTTP/1.1" 200 87872 "http://www.mooreds.com" "DuckDuckBot/1.0;
(+http://duckduckgo.com/duckduckbot.html)"
185.24.234.106 - - [26/Jul/2019:20:20:50 -0600] "GET /wordpress/archives/
date/2004/08 HTTP/1.1" 200 81183 "http://www.mooreds.com" "DuckDuckBot/1.0;
(+http://duckduckgo.com/duckduckbot.html)"
```

awk

awk is a multipurpose line processing utility. I often want to refine the data in a log file to highlight certain aspects. This helps me figure out what's going on.

For example, if we want to see only the IP addresses (the first string in the line which looks like 54.147.20.92) from the file in Listing 4-1, we can use awk to extract that field. awk uses numbers to reference the position in the line, so the IP address is $1. You can see in Listing 4-2 that only the IP addresses are printed.

Listing 4-2. *The awk command and output to print IP addresses*

```
$ awk '{print $1}' logs.txt
54.147.20.92
185.24.234.106
185.24.234.106
```

You can pull out specific fields, or you can print rows with fields that match a certain string. You can sum up values of numeric fields. awk is on every modern Unix system and is useful for such field extraction or manipulation.

sed

sed is another utility that operates on each line of a file. I typically use it to search and replace text in a file. Let's process the log file in Listing 4-1 to anonymize the IP address and the user agent (the string that contains the name of the program which retrieved the web page, like "Slackbot"). Perhaps we're going to ship the log file to long-term storage and are concerned about users' privacy. Using sed, we can easily remove this sensitive data, as seen in Listing 4-3.

Listing 4-3. Removing fields using sed

```
$ sed 's/^[^ ]*//' logs.txt |sed 's/"[^"]*"$//'
- - [26/Jul/2019:20:21:04 -0600] "GET /wordpress HTTP/1.1" 301 241 "-"
- -  [26/Jul/2019:20:20:50  -0600]  "GET  /wordpress/archives/date/2004/02
HTTP/1.1" 200 87872 "http://www.mooreds.com"
- -  [26/Jul/2019:20:20:50  -0600]  "GET  /wordpress/archives/date/2004/08
HTTP/1.1" 200 81183 "http://www.mooreds.com"
```

Yes, the strings like 's/^[^]*//' may look like line noise, but this is a regular expression. I won't talk much about regular expressions, but they are present in every modern language and let you match and modify text easily. sed gives you the power of regular expressions at the command line to process text files.

jq

If you work with modern software, chances are you have encountered JSON. It's used for configuration, web API requests, and log files. Sometimes you need to parse JSON and extract part of the data. Tools like sed and awk are suboptimal for this task because they expect newlines to separate records, not curly braces and commas. Sure, you could use regular expressions to parse simple JSON; I've done this in a pinch. But using jq is a far superior experience. I use it whenever I am working with an API that returns JSON. I can retrieve the API with curl (another great CLI tool) and parse it with jq.

If the processing is in any way complicated, I put these commands in a script and then I can repeat my use of this API easily.

A few months ago, I was exploring the Elasticsearch API. I crafted the queries with curl and then used jq to parse the results so I could understand them. Yes, I could have done this same API exploration with a programming language like Python or Ruby, but it would have taken longer. I could also have used a GUI tool like Postman, but then it would have been harder to repeat and refine the process.

sed and awk should be on every system you run across; jq is not usually installed but is a single, free, stand-alone downloadable binary.

Spend time getting to know these tools. Next time you extract information from a text file, reach for sed or awk. If you need to pull out the third element of the objects with a 'foo' key from a JSON file, look to jq. I think you'll be happy with the results.

Sincerely,

Dan

Version control

Dear new developer,

If in doubt, put it under version control.

Version control lets you keep track of the nuts and bolts of a software system, the files which contain the code and logic. Keeping these under version control lets you make changes. If you screw things up, you can roll back to working code. Version control also lets you see who made what changes when to which files. When you need to find out who to ask about the bizarre function in class XYZ, you can. By the way, don't be surprised if that person is you—that's happened to me before.

There are many version control systems. What you use should depend on your needs, but one determinant is how many people interact with your codebase. These days you'll likely use a distributed version control system like git or mercurial. But any version control system, even a crufty old one like RCS or CVS, is far better than nothing.

Version control systems can be expensive, but some are free. If you aren't using anything to version control your code, please start. The easiest way is to use a hosted service. GitHub, Bitbucket, and GitLab all are online services with free tiers; they are happy to store your codebase for you. Learning one of the modern version control systems will help on the job, because running a software project of any size without version control is a rare, foolhardy endeavor.

If you are on a team that doesn't use version control, you can still use it yourself. In this situation, you don't want to use a hosted service, since you could inadvertently expose proprietary code without the organization's consent—that can get you fired. Instead, use one of the free systems hosted on your development computer. This will be more work, as you'll have to sync between the existing system and your version controlled code, but if you can see exactly when a bug was added, or when you need to roll back to the way the code was a week ago, it'll be worth the effort. Hopefully, you can show the power of a version control system to others, and it will spread to the rest of the team.

An alternative, of course, is to find another job. I honestly can't think of a good reason to avoid version control. I only have seen this when working with people who lacked basic software development skills and had just hacked a system together.

There are some items that don't belong in version control, however. Large files, text or binary, belong on a file system or object store like AWS S3. Structured data should be stored in a database. Sensitive information, such as passwords, belongs in a secrets manager. Documents that are going to be edited by nontechnical users should be stored in a document repository.

But everything else, all the source code and build scripts, all the infrastructure setup and developer documentation, all the CSS files and SQL scripts—all this should be kept in a version control system. The code and supporting files that need to be processed to build your application should be stored in version control.

Sincerely,

Dan

Text editors

Dear new developer,

The raw "stuff" of software is usually text files. Well, to be honest, the foundation of software is ideas and insight, but unfortunately, a server can't yet run on those. So, you must create text files.

One straightforward way to do that is to use a piece of software called a text editor. This program is designed solely to manipulate text. If you have used TextEdit on a Mac or Notepad on a Windows PC, you have used a text editor.

Why a text editor rather than an integrated development environment (also called an IDE)? An IDE combines a text editor with tools that perform other development functions such as testing and debugging. Text editors can be used for any language, whereas IDEs focus on one or a few. Text editors can run almost anywhere, whereas IDEs usually run on your local development computer. Using a text editor will also help you to become more familiar with the command line. In the end, text editors are more flexible than IDEs.

For those reasons, it's better to start with a text editor than an IDE. There are many options. Two good ones, with long lineages, a cost of zero dollars, and copious functionality, are vi and emacs. But there are plenty of other options. Most text editors are extendable, and you can plug in features such as syntax highlighting, which lets you know when you misspell a language keyword; it's worth spending time researching and installing such extensions.

What if you learn the wrong text editor? "What if I learn the wrong XYZ?" is a question you'll face many times as a developer. Since you don't know the future, you're always gambling when you invest your time to learn anything. But every time you learn one tool or technology, you will have more context and understanding about that class of tools or technologies. For example, learning vi will make it easier to pick up the next text editor, map its functionality to what you know, and become productive. You also learn the jargon around the technology or tool, which makes it far easier to use a search engine to solve problems.

Text editors are easy to learn, but difficult to master. Opening a file, typing text, and saving the file shouldn't take long to learn. But to be able to easily navigate between files, move around within a file, or do a mass search and replace, you're going to have to put in some effort.

There is no more widely available, widely applicable way to convert thoughts into files than a text editor.

Sincerely,

Dan

IDEs

Dear new developer,

Just as you should learn a text editor, you should learn an integrated development environment (IDE). This is a stand-alone program which helps you write code in one or more languages. They typically range in cost from free to a couple of hundred bucks.

Wait, didn't I tell you that a text editor was superior to an IDE?

Context is crucial. If you are writing Java code on your laptop, using an IDE will be a superior experience. If you are editing and recompiling Java files to rebuild jar files in order to debug a production issue on the server—an unpleasant experience I have done more than once—a text editor is better. Using an IDE when you need to modify files on a remote server will require syncing files between the server and your development environment.

Using an IDE will give you the following benefits:

- It will be easier to navigate a project. IDEs usually have a tree view of the entire project. If you are not familiar with the command line, having this view will make it easier for you to see how the project fits together. If the language supports it, an IDE can provide powerful searching capabilities allowing you to see where a function, method, or class is referenced.

- Often these programs have refactoring support. Refactoring allows you to rename files, variables, functions, and methods. If the language or IDE supports it, all references to the renamed entity can be updated as well. This lets you rename parts of your codebase when their purpose changes and be confident you aren't breaking anything.

- IDEs have integrated debugging and code inspection capabilities. You can walk through code running locally and see the values of variables. You can call functions. You can also, if the language supports it, connect to remote servers and examine the state of a program running there.

- The IDE can provide text manipulation beyond refactoring. For instance, if you want to add a documentation section to every method or generate boilerplate functions, most IDEs let you do this with a couple of keystrokes.

- An IDE can make it easier to learn a language or framework. If you are not sure of the exact name or syntax of a library call, an IDE can suggest it. This suggestion is usually based on the first few letters you type. The system documentation can be displayed at the same time. For example, if you are using an IDE for Java development, you can usually see documentation for a method by mousing over it.

As you see in the preceding list, an IDE is a powerful way to interact with a codebase. It is also tied to a language's features. If you are using a dynamically typed language such as PHP or Ruby, your IDE will have different capabilities than if you are using a statically typed language like C# or Java. But in either case, mastering your IDE will make it easier to write and debug code.

Sincerely,

Dan

The standard library

Dear new developer,

If you want to be good at *interviews*, learn your algorithms. Many companies use algorithm knowledge as a proxy for general problem-solving ability. If you squint, it makes a sort of sense—you have to break down a problem into pieces, turn each into a set of steps, and implement it in code. You can brush up on algorithms at places like HackerRank. Like any proxy, algorithm knowledge can be gamed, which is why tech interviewing feels like a fundamentally broken process. But I digress.

If you want to be good at your *job*, learn your standard library. This is the omnipresent set of functions or classes that your code can use to accomplish tasks while executing. You can use it for simple things, like a list to store variables, or for complex tasks such as generating a random number or encrypting data.

Every modern language has a definition (this includes syntax and keywords) and a set of associated, standardized classes or functions. These classes or functions allow developers to "stand on the shoulders of giants" and should be used whenever possible.

Why? These libraries evolve over time as the language improves. They have the following benefits:

- Using the standard library lets you accelerate development. You don't have to roll your own hash or binary tree, just use the one that ships with your library. You can be assured it'll be available when your program executes.

- Standard libraries have a lot of eyes on them looking for issues. This means that edge cases and security bugs are discovered without effort on your part. If the concerns are serious, they will be fixed quickly.

- Any developer who joins your company is going to be more familiar with the standard library than they will be with any internal libraries. Using the standard library means new team members are more effective faster.

- A standard library has many developers improving it. While it's difficult to get exact numbers for such contributions, according to GitHub Golang has had over 1500 contributors to the project[1] and PHP has had over 700.[2] This leads to security and performance gains over time. And you'll often get the benefits of these changes with a simple library upgrade.

In general, many more engineers work on and with standard libraries than work on the code in your company.

To get these benefits, you must know and use the standard library. However, unlike the syntax of a language, you don't need to know it to get things done. While you can't roll up your sleeves and start coding until you know the syntax of a language like Ruby, Haskell, or JavaScript, you can ship a lot of code

---

[1] https://github.com/golang/go
[2] https://github.com/php/php-src

without knowing the ins and outs of the standard library. You must make a conscious choice to utilize the standard library in your code to get the benefits.

Standard libraries can be large: Java has thousands of classes in its standard library. Even a language with a relatively small standard library such as JavaScript has approximately 70 objects, many with tens of properties or methods. These libraries take time to learn. Plus, new developer, it can feel like you're not doing much when you are reading docs. Certainly, reading isn't as fun as banging out code.

There are also large community-supported codebases augmenting standard libraries for many languages. Sometimes they are centralized, like CPAN (the Comprehensive Perl Archive Network) for Perl and CRAN (the Comprehensive R Archive Network) for R. Code from these sources share many aspects of the language's standard library. It's a good idea to evaluate these packages when you are building software. But be aware that there are wildly varying levels of support for community packages, ranging from very active to unmaintained. Make sure you understand the license granting you the use of packages and what that means if you use them.

If you read the standard library documentation and start using it in your code, there will be two benefits for your software:

- You will save time in developing and your code will be better; see the reasons mentioned above. You'll permanently raise your abilities in that language for the rest of your career.

- You will write idiomatic code. Other developers who are familiar with the standard library will know the characteristics and behavior of the software you write.

and a large benefit for you and your career:

- You will gain a transferable skill set. Learning how to use the custom Ruby libraries that your company created is not as valuable to other companies as your knowledge of the standard Ruby library.

How can you learn the standard library? I'd recommend taking a high-level overflight. Search for "<language> standard library overview" and get reading. I'd also recommend scanning the documentation and seeing what piques your interest—data structures, high-level flow control, or specialty functions. This overview is partly about you being aware of available options and partly about you learning the terms used so that you'll be a better searcher.

After you have that overview, the best way to learn the standard library is to use it. When you confront a problem, check the standard library docs to see if it has already been solved. Make that a regular part of your development process; make a habit of asking yourself "Is there a standard library function for that?" Your code will improve. You'll also learn when to venture beyond the library.

If you have time and inclination, you can also search for "<language> koans." A programming koan is a small exercise problem in a certain language. These are great ways to practice and explore the standard library in a low-risk environment.

When "there is more than one way to do it" using a standard library, which happens more in some languages (like PHP) than in others (like Golang), evaluate options and then be consistent within your codebase.

Learn the standard library. Make the time.

Sincerely,

Dan

Automated testing

Dear new developer,

If you want to build great software systems, learn automated testing. Depending on your platform of choice, you may have built-in options, or you may need to investigate and select a testing framework. A test suite protects your code the same way Styrofoam peanuts protect the delicate contents of a shipped package. Sure, your code can still break, but it's less likely to do so.

Automated tests are code and that means there is a maintenance cost. Both the infrastructure to execute the tests and the developer time spent keeping the test code up to date are expenses. I once worked on a project that had so many tests that any change to the code consisted mostly of updating the tests. However, test code doesn't need to be the same quality as production code. Practices that are red flags in production code, like code duplication and unhandled exceptions, are more acceptable in test code; it is supporting infrastructure.

However, paying this cost has benefits. On that project with the abundance of tests, we knew when code changes broke the system. We regularly changed complicated logic knowing that if behavior changed, even of unlikely edge cases, the tests would flag it and let us know.

On a different project, I wrote many tests around a payment processing subsystem. Every time there was a bug, I wrote a test for it. Then I knew I'd never release that bug to my users again. That's one of the biggest wins for testing: automated tests prevent regressions. It is not very much fun for anyone, user or developer, to have a bug fixed but then have it pop up six months down the line. Writing a test for every bug fix prevents this.

When you run them regularly, tests are living documentation. Set up continuous integration to do so. Such tests help new developers get up to speed on a project. The new developer can tweak a program and get instant feedback, rather than having to find the precise set of steps to take in an application to exercise that bit of code.

It takes a while to understand the right way to test. There are plenty of books to read. My experience is less theoretical and mostly "on the ground." In my experience:

- Unit test any logic that is complicated or subject to regular change.

- Integration testing is great at making sure components work together.

- Know what your language or framework provides and prefer that.

- Use a continuous integration tool to run tests on every branch.

However, every codebase has different constraints. The most important thing is to start—don't let the perfect be the enemy of the good.

I remember the moment I realized the value of automated testing. I was managing a team that, among other responsibilities, operated an ingest engine for real estate data. Releasing this software was a three-day process which included manually evaluating data in the staging and production databases to ensure no regressions occurred. We added testing into the process and were able to release in minutes with high confidence. It was a game changer.

Don't try to test all user interfaces using automated testing. Instead, focus on the important ones. Automated testing of user interfaces is slow and often leads to breaking tests as the interface changes.

If you are beginning to implement automated testing, start with pure stateless business logic. Functions that do simple and stateless things like split strings are a great place to start, because you can easily write a unit test and make sure your code handles edge cases. For example, a string splitting function must handle null strings, empty strings, or strings with the delimiter missing. However, before you write any particular function, check your standard library to see if it's already been implemented for you.

To repeat, just start. If you have a project with no testing, make the initial investment and write the first test, even if it is trivial: "Can I instantiate this object?" With that infrastructure in place, writing any other test is now easier.

Force yourself to write tests even when you're slinging a lot of code. It will help the future you, I promise.

Sincerely,

Dan

Network engineering

Allan Wintersieck is the CTO and cofounder of Devetry, a software consultancy in Denver that provides strategic partnership for software architecture and engineering.

Dear new developer,

I realize that just trying to learn basic programming principles can feel daunting enough, but if I may, I'd recommend adding one more task to your list: learn a little bit about network engineering.

Networking underpins everything web and app developers do, since almost every web app communicates from the front end to the back end regularly. Most developers understand the basics of making API calls and how data flows over the Internet, but taking a small dive deeper will help you debug issues for years to come.

The goal is to build your underlying knowledge so that when you encounter related issues in the future, you understand enough about how it all works to intelligently tackle the problem. For example, the reason everyone complains about CORS (Cross-Origin Resource Sharing) being confusing is because it doesn't make sense without first understanding the basic principles of networking and security.

Here is a quick list to get you started:

- Read up on the basics of routing. No need to dive into how the protocols work but understand why it's set up this way and how Internet traffic gets to where it needs to go.

- Read the basics of DNS and understand how a DNS request is resolved.

- Read a brief rundown of the OSI model. Focus on understanding one or two examples of things you've dealt with in the past that exist at each layer.

- Review the difference between TCP/IP and HTTP and why they exist at different layers in the model.

- Read up on the basics of what a "proxy" is.

An overall analogy that I find helpful: Networking is like sending mail via the postal service.

- Routing is the process of putting mail in your mailbox, having a postal worker pick it up, and it eventually reaching its destination.

- DNS is the process of looking up someone's mailing address so you can send them mail.

- The OSI model is a fancy name for making it clear that there's a lot of details the postal service takes care of for us. Most people understand how addresses and mailboxes work (let's call that the equivalent to the Application layer), but don't really understand all the internal details of how the postal service gets your mail to its destination. All those details are the first six layers of the model.

With that background knowledge in place, tackle some of these additional questions to lead you to more learning:

- How do CDNs (Content Delivery Networks) work?

- What's the difference between "regular" HTTP and WebSockets?

- How does SSL (HTTPS vs. HTTP) work, at a high level?

- What can nginx be used for?

And as a last exercise, sketch out a complete picture of a work app or side project: what DNS calls get made, what servers are involved, are there any proxies, what protocols are in use, what OSI layer those protocols exist on, and so on.

I promise that spending the first few years of my career as a network engineer only slightly biases me toward learning this stuff.

Sincerely,

Allan Wintersieck

SQL

Dear new developer,

It's a good idea to learn SQL, which stands for "Structured Query Language." SQL lets you interact with relational databases. Relational databases are very good at storing a wide variety of types of data. These database systems are mature, well documented, and performant. They are easy to scale and operate. Sure, at the far edges of speed, scale, and functionality, there are other data store options, but in general you should reach for such solutions when a relational database falls short, not before.

You use SQL to retrieve or modify data by writing queries. These queries will pull or update specific rows of data, rows that match a certain set of parameters, or perhaps aggregate data across a query. For example, if you have table of orders, you could write a query to pull order #1, orders to be shipped today, or to find the sum of the value of all orders this month.

As a new developer, you don't need to be a SQL expert. It is a mind-expanding way to interact with data. Instead of being procedural, object oriented, or functional like most programming languages, SQL is set based. I confess I've been using it for decades and still haven't mastered it.

There are often frameworks that sit between you and the relational database your application uses for data storage, such as ActiveRecord for Rails, Hibernate for Java, or SQLAlchemy for Python. These frameworks make simple operations simpler. If you want to look a record up via an id or run a simple query, these tools make it a snap. But if you need to join across multiple tables or leverage database-specific functions, the abstraction often breaks down. This is where knowing SQL is useful.

There are also queries for which a framework is too slow. For example, if you wanted to sum a set of orders in a day to get a daily total, a naive framework would load all the data for the orders and then sum up the order value in memory, possibly using too much. A more sophisticated framework would generate SQL summing up the values. Unfortunately, it's hard to know whether the framework you are using is naive or sophisticated without examining the SQL it generates. Dropping into SQL always works. However, you shouldn't optimize for performance until you have found this to be a bottleneck.

Some systems or frameworks seem mysterious, but at the end of the day, the magic is built on code and data storage. By looking at the underlying data storage, you can understand what these frameworks take care of. For a long time, Rails migrations seemed magical to me. When I looked at the database, it became clear that Rails migrations were built on storing the date/time portion of the migration name in the schema_migrations table. Now, when Rails migrations are in a weird state, which happens sometimes when I run migrations, switch version control branches, and then rerun migrations, I can fix the issue by tweaking the underlying table. It's good to be able to peel back the abstraction. SQL helps you do that.

To learn SQL, you can install a SQL database on your computer and play around with it. SQLite is the easiest system to install, but MySQL or PostgreSQL are more likely to be used in your day-to-day work. It's also worth reading the reference documentation for your database of choice.

Some people have strong opinions on the type of SQL database they use, whether a commercial offering like SQL Server or Oracle or an open source solution like MySQL or PostgreSQL. As a new developer, you want to learn whatever your company is using. The difference between them when you are running basic queries isn't much. The databases have larger differences in advanced SQL functions and performance and administration concerns. That'll matter later in your career.

Sincerely,

Dan

Debuggers

Dear new developer,

When you are fixing a bug in a program, you must understand its state. A bug is any undesired or unexpected behavior in a program—the term comes from a moth which caused an issue in an early computer.[3] This state includes user input, values from a persistent data store, and nondeterministic state like the current time. But the most important state is the in-memory representation of the code. What function or procedure is executing when the bug appears and what did all the variables look like at that moment?

Reproducing a problem with a test or replication sequence is the first step to solving the issue. Ensure that your debugging environment is as similar as possible to the environment in which the problem appears. I remember one program I was debugging which worked fine in development but failed miserably in production. The application used Google Web Toolkit, which compiled Java to JavaScript. When I compiled the application in development, the obfuscated variable names were different. That ended up being the root issue—there was a variable name collision between the compiled JavaScript and an incorrectly namespaced JavaScript variable. I tore my hair out and was reduced to putting in `console.log` statements on production to debug the issue.

That's how a lot of debugging happens—printing out log statements to a file. You can solve many problems that way, it's extremely portable and customizable, and it gives you at least *some* insight into program state.

However, a far better solution is to use a debugger. They've been around since the 1980s and give you more flexible insight into a program's in-memory state than logging. You can see the value of any variable. You can run commands interactively. You can stop the flow of a program and restart it. If you pair an

---

[3] `http://ei.cs.vt.edu/~history/Hopper.Danis.html`

interactive debugger with an automated test, you have a tight feedback loop to help you zero in on the bug.

Most languages have interactive debuggers. In fact, that's a way to decide which languages to avoid; a programming language without a debugger is likely to have other issues, such as a substandard dependency management system. Some languages have standard protocols which you can use to connect to remote servers. You run the debugger on your own system, but can examine the state from the remote server. If you ever need to debug a production issue, having this available is wonderful.

Debuggers are often integrated with an IDE, but some are run on the command line. Whatever your language, search for "<language> debugger" and find out more about this valuable tool.

Sincerely,

Dan

Benchmarking

Dear new developer,

Don't worry about creating fast code until you need it. If you write code expressly to run quickly, you will write code that is hard to maintain. Err on the side of writing code that is easy to understand.

But there are times when performance really matters. When this is the case, reach for a benchmarking tool first, before you optimize anything. This will let you examine the performance characteristics of your code in a replicable way.

For instance, if you wanted to know whether it was faster to execute a function or a lambda in Ruby, you could use the code in Listing 4-4.

Listing 4-4. Benchmarking Ruby code

```
require 'benchmark'
def test_function(a,b)
  return a+b
end

my_lambda = lambda {|a,b| return a+b }

puts "testing function performance"
puts Benchmark.measure {
  50_000_000.times do
my_function(rand, rand)
  end
}
```

```
puts "testing lambda performance"
puts Benchmark.measure {
  50_000_000.times do
my_lambda.call(rand, rand)
  end
}
```

It doesn't really matter what a lambda is in this case. What's important is that this code runs two different, logically equivalent, code paths 50 million times. It then prints the execution duration. You can benchmark function executions, website page response time, database queries, or microservice calls.

Benchmarking provides concrete numbers reflecting how changes to your code affect run duration. This is crucial to making progress on performance issues. Whenever someone says "this is too slow," reach for your benchmarking tools to quantify what "too slow" means. Then run them when you make changes to ensure you're not making a bad problem worse.

Sincerely,

Dan

Search engines

Dear new developer,

Web search engines are important tools for building modern software. On the other hand, search engines are less useful for building foundational software knowledge, simply because you don't know what to search for. Books, video classes, or side projects are better, depending on how you learn. Searching is tough if you don't know what terms to use. Once you know a bit of software jargon, searching the Web lets you leverage the freely shared knowledge of others.

When searching, search for the exact error message (almost). When you get an error message like nginx_1 | 2019/01/06 20:42:22 [crit] 11#11: *1 connect() to unix:/var/run/php5-fpm.sock failed (13: Permission denied), don't just cut and paste it into the search box. Examine the error message and see what in the error message is unique and what is common to all errors of this type. For the preceding error message, text like the nginx instance name, nginx_1, and the date and time are unique. Searching on them won't be very useful. But the message text starting with connect() seems less unique. Searching on that string has a higher chance of yielding good results.

Read the results carefully, whether a blog post, Stack Overflow answer, or project documentation. I've been bitten by this more times than I care to remember. It's easy when you find a result that seems to solve the issue to cut and paste the top answer and return to what you were doing before you were blocked. A better choice is to read the entire page or even multiple pages of results to make sure what you found solves your problem. Pick the best solution; this may not be the first one, especially if the first result is old. While newer releases often resolve existing problems, upgrading has its own risks. Read the release notes and make an informed choice.

Reviewing more than just the first result also builds your knowledge base. Doing a search should help you beyond simply answering your immediate question. You want to learn about the issue and solution in a broader context. This will help you incorporate what you've learned into your mental model. This means that next time you will know better what to search and may not need to search at all. You're building foundational knowledge at the same time as you solve your immediate problem. Trying to understand various solutions and what they are doing is a way to do just-in-time learning. Mindlessly copying the solution isn't.

Add links to what you find in your commits and code comments, especially if the solution is esoteric. Write a commit message that explains your intent, with the link providing additional context.

Think about the terms you use in the search query. Choosing the terms is where foundational knowledge of your problem space is critical. For example, if you know that ActiveRecord is an object-relational mapping tool, or that Ruby is a dynamic language where every class can change another, a procedure called "monkey patching," then you know how to search for these concepts and related knowledge. If you want to change a specific ActiveRecord behavior, you might search for "how to monkeypatch active record" which will get you far more useful results than "how do I change the rails database access system." This process is iterative. Pay attention to the terms used in helpful content and use them in new queries.

Finally, search engines work well because there's information produced by people like you and me. You can take part in producing that content, either by asking or answering questions on Stack Overflow, writing a blog post, or responding to a forum post. If you encounter an issue no one has ever seen before, write up your solution. Participation in the wider Internet is crucial for its continuing usefulness. So, take part and give back.

Sincerely,

Dan

The keyboard

Dear new developer,

Software engineering is so much more than typing on a keyboard. Other things that matter include:

- Knowing who to talk to
- Determining what to build
- Abstract ideas
- Concrete details
- Testing and documentation
- Communicating progress
- Course correcting when a project goes awry

These are all skills you need to be a great developer. However, knowing how to type quickly will make you a better developer too.

Touch typing is one way to do this; it is the ability to type without looking at the keyboard with all ten of your fingers. If you don't have use of all your fingers or you use fewer, you can still type quickly, as a study from Aalto University found in 2016.[4]

Typing quickly is important because many forms of developer communication are text based, such as chat, email, or ticketing systems. Being a fast typer will allow you to write code more quickly as well. For the same reasons, you should learn keyboard shortcuts for your commonly used programs.

You can Google "practice touch typing" and find many places to improve your speed. There are also competitions like typeracer. I was lucky enough to learn to touch type in school, so I haven't had to use any of these.

However!

If I had to choose between being a fast typer who didn't understand a problem space or a slow typer who did, I'd pick the latter every time. Often, the best code is no code. Focus on understanding a problem first and then solving it.

That is to say, make sure your fast typing solves the correct problem.

Sincerely,

Dan

---

[4]www.aalto.fi/en/news/ten-fingers-not-needed-for-fast-typing

In conclusion

Part of your job as a software developer is keeping track of tools and the increased leverage they provide. You must balance between evaluating new tools to solve problems faster and chasing endlessly after newly released shiny languages, frameworks, or libraries.

However, software developers are lucky. Unlike many other professionals, our tools cost nothing to copy. This means that many tools are distributed at zero cost and require nothing more than an investment of time. Once you make the investment to learn a tool well, you'll reap the benefits of increased productivity for the rest of your career.

Practices

According to the dictionary, a practice is a repeated or customary action or the usual way of doing something.

In this chapter, I'll share some of the practices that help me be a better developer. Some may be surprising. Others may appear to be common sense. With repetition and time, each of these practices will make you a more effective software engineer.

Just like starting a new hobby or starting to exercise, take it easy. Don't try to pick up all of these at once. Choose one that makes sense to you and, well, "practice" it. After you feel comfortable with that one, choose another.

Don't just write code—solve problems

Dear new developer,

It's a paradox, but sometimes you provide the most value by *not* writing code. Remember, your job is problem-solving, not building software. Custom code can have tremendous value but comes with costs:

- It needs to be deployed, maintained, and upgraded.
- It has bugs.
- Logic changes require a developer.
- It has opportunity cost; accomplishing task A with code means that you might not have time to accomplish task B.

© Dan Moore 2020
D. Moore, *Letters to a New Developer*, https://doi.org/10.1007/978-1-4842-6074-6_5

I aim to solve problems without code whenever possible. This is a mindset that I picked up at a job because there were too many problems and not enough developers. I started to look around at ways to let my nontechnical colleagues overcome their roadblocks and realized that using such tools gave me more leverage too.

Here are a few ways you might solve a business problem writing little or no software:

- *Use a library or framework*—I worked at a place where they had written their own database connection pool. Why? I never got an answer, but from what I saw, one of the open source solutions would have worked just as well. Be on the lookout for open source projects and tools that you can suggest when someone considers writing low-level solutions like that connection pool.

- *Use a third-party SaaS tool*—I have seen companies run their own git repositories. Now, there may be good reasons to do this, such as security or privacy concerns. But GitHub has a better developer experience and likely a better security infrastructure. If you want to suggest one of these tools, make sure you understand the problem, available solutions, and ongoing costs.

- *Deprioritize the work*—Once I met with my CEO to discuss integrating outside data sources to improve our product. I asked why we thought the additional effort was worthwhile. We were considering this work only because we'd done it in the past. In other words, inertia—not generally a good reason for a business decision. We prioritized other work instead. If you want to avoid useless or lower-value work, have a clear road map and a willingness to ask questions.

- *Do the work manually*—I was working on a startup, and we occasionally refunded customers. I could have written custom code to automatically process these refunds. But it was much easier to document the process and refund customers manually. The refunds happened rarely enough that automation wasn't worth it. If you are considering a manual process, understand how often the process will need to be done, the amount of effort involved, and if growth will change either.

Now, new developer, sometimes you may not understand the larger context of your work. You may propose a noncode solution that isn't the right fit. Writing code can solve a problem quite elegantly and may be the best solution.

Whenever I'm not sure I fully understand a situation, I confess my ignorance before I make suggestions. I might say something like "I am not sure I have the full picture, but I think we could solve <the business problem> using solution A or project B, rather than writing our own code." If you are working directly with a client, they won't care, as long as the problem is solved. If you are on a team, the lead engineer or project manager should have a good understanding of alternatives and why custom code is the right solution. They should be happy to share that reasoning with you.

Practice solving business problems, rather than writing code.

Sincerely,

Dan

Look around corners

Dear new developer,

Just like chess players think many moves ahead, consider the ramifications of your choices. Thinking about consequences will help you make better decisions. Strive to plan out two, three, or more steps.

And don't just plan for the happy, straightforward path to success. Practice looking around corners, thinking about what might go wrong.

I was chatting with an acquaintance about technology choices at his employer. He referred to the "original sin" of choosing a NoSQL database as their primary data store. This decision had ripple effects that lasted years, affecting features, teams, and timelines. This early choice constrained future options for dozens of developers. You may not be making the kind of choice that influences teams for years, but your technical decisions also constrain options.

The biggest decisions are platform choices, such as Rails or Django, Java or Golang, MySQL or PostgreSQL. But even smaller choices have ripple effects. I can't count the number of times I've said to myself "Oh, I'll just upgrade this *one* thing; it won't be hard." That component upgrade cascades, requiring other changes. When I recognize this, I can abort, commit, or pause and discuss. But in all these cases, I would have been better off considering the possible scenarios before starting.

Think through the ramifications—practice imagining what might go right and what might go wrong. For example, someone might say "we want to allow people to change their email address." Okay. What if a user's email address is the primary key of a table? What if the email address connects user data across accounts? This change may be more difficult than you thought.

I'm not saying don't change. That way lies madness—and COBOL. I'm also not saying you should overengineer and write code for every eventuality. YAGNI[1] is a common expression among developers for a reason.

Rather, consider how simple changes in complicated systems often ripple out and cause unexpected havoc. Planning how to test, mitigate, or handle this is a good way to avoid unpleasant surprises.

You can't know what lies around every corner. But that doesn't mean you should pretend there are no corners.

Sincerely,

Dan

Read code

Dear new developer,

Coding is fun. You take an idea, breathe life into it, and have a finished product that people can interact with. Software development is an amazing occupation, and you can build tools that change the world.

However, code is read more often than it is written. Why? Because reading the code is the first step to understanding it and changing it. Furthermore:

- *Companies pay for code*—Code is expensive. Companies don't like to spend more money than they must. They want to amortize the expense of code across as many years as they can. This means you often change existing code rather than write new code.

- *Bugs happen*—The software is almost correct, but not quite. Anyone fixing a bug must understand the existing code and how it works.

- *Business requirements change*—Code that supports the business needs to change as well. But before that, the developer modifying the code must understand how it currently works. New features should also integrate with existing structures.

Over the years the business commits to a codebase, there will be many changes and bug fixes.

---

[1]You Aren't Gonna Need It: https://en.wikipedia.org/wiki/You_aren%27t_gonna_need_it

There is the rare piece of software that is "set and forget." It hums along quietly with no changes. I was responsible for such a system; it ran for five years with zero changes as it sent email alerts about new houses for sale. Different industries have different software longevity. But even in government, where systems live for decades, code still changes.

As a new developer, you will mostly likely spend more time trying to understand existing code, to debug or change it, than writing new code. Of course, this ratio depends on what your company needs. A startup with a great idea and nothing else will require a greater portion of time spent writing software than an established business. But even in a startup, once you acquire users, you begin the maintenance phase where bug fixes and reading code take a greater and greater share of your time.

What does that mean for you? Practice reading code. When I need to make changes to an unfamiliar project, I read the code in the following ways:

- *I scan*—I'm seeking a high-level overview. This information should be written down, but sometimes needs to be extracted from someone's brain or from the code. In the latter cases, document what you learn. I'm trying to answer the following questions:

  - What problem does this code try to solve?

  - What language and/or framework is it using?

  - Is it written idiomatically?

  - What are the main components of the application?

  - How do they fit together?

- *I dive down*—I focus on the problem at hand and try to identify where changes should be made. This usually involves opening source files and moving between them, trying to understand the logic of this subsystem. I also look for patterns in the code, including different levels of abstraction, homegrown libraries or frameworks, and coding idioms. Consistency matters so I want to learn the style of the codebase.

- *I use the scientific method*—I write a hypothesis in a text file or notebook, make small changes, and see what happens. All the better if you can make changes in a staging system or in a development environment. Automated tests are helpful in verifying my theories and in making sure I don't inadvertently change something else. If you can't make a local copy of the entire application, you can still run chunks of code locally to get a better understanding of what the system is doing.

Beware of the temptation to try to read and understand the entire system before making any changes. That will lead to paralysis. How much you need to understand depends on:

- How encapsulated the component or system is. Will changes there ripple out? Or are there clear boundaries?

- Is the code you're changing well tested? Or untested?

- How critical is this area of the codebase and the larger system? The more important, the more you'll want to understand it before modifying it.

Discuss these questions with your team. But realize an understanding of the entire system only comes with time.

Also, ignore any desire to throw away old code and rewrite it, especially if you don't understand it. Old code is reified knowledge, and you discard it at your peril. There is a time to junk old systems. When you don't understand what they do is not it.

Software systems spend most of their life running in production. Change happens, but that requires understanding what is already present. This means reading code is more important than writing code.

Sincerely,

Dan

Estimate your work

Dear new developer,

Knowing how long it will take to build software is almost as important as being able to build it. Web page, component, entire software subsystem, it doesn't matter—as soon as your organization decides to build it, a pressing question will be "how long will it take?" This process is known as estimation. It's difficult but you can get better with practice.

Estimation is important for three reasons. The first is opportunity cost. Each feature built necessarily excludes creating a different one. Both the costs and benefits of each effort must be evaluated and prioritized to build those of the highest value first. The length of time it takes to build software is a key component of its cost.

Another reason is scheduling. Very often software teams need to deliver based on external deadlines. These can be hard, fixed deadlines, such as the date of a trade show or a customer commitment, or softer, such as an internal road map commitment or a promise to another team. Delivering on time lets other parties execute their own plans. Software isn't built in a vacuum.

Now, of course, as Dwight Eisenhower, former President of the United States, said:

> In preparing for battle I have always found that plans are useless, but planning is indispensable.

The value of estimates is not only prioritization and scheduling—these often shift over time. Stuff happens, estimates get pushed, priorities reworked.

The third reason to estimate is that the team is forced to plan. This leads to discussions and questions about requirements and implementation details. Such planning forces you to think concretely about what you are building and the trade-offs you will have to make. These discussions inform and change the software. Changes at this time should be welcomed, as they are far easier to make before any code has been written.

I have tried to define requirements for a system and build it at the same time. This ended up costing more money and taking more time than if we had done a detailed estimation session. If a client needs to see a solution before they "get" it and can have a discussion about the requirements, use lightweight prototyping tools to avoid writing software.

New developer, there are many ways to estimate. Following team practices ensures consistency.

However, the following is an example of an estimation process that has worked for me. When I was a consultant, I did the following:

- Wrote a task list for the project. Everything I could possibly imagine needing to deliver the final product would go on the list: requirements definition, research, development, testing, deployment, even a ballpark guess on bug fixing. I wanted to be as thorough as possible.

- Put the list in a spreadsheet with four columns, as seen in Table 5-1.

- Add a high and low estimate to each task. Specify both in ideal hours; six ideal hours per day was my rule of thumb.

- The low estimate was how long the task would take if it went perfectly—no questions, no changes, no unpleasant surprises, just understanding the task and executing.

- The high estimate was how long the task would take if things went sideways—if, for example, I ran into an obstacle and had to rebuild an entire component.

- If you are on a team, you may want to use days or half days rather than hours, but I wouldn't use larger units than that. I don't know anyone who can reliably estimate software tasks in units of weeks. It simply isn't granular enough. If this is a large project, estimates will get rolled up into weeks or months— just don't use those units of time for task estimation.

- Add any questions uncovered or assumptions made during the task time estimate to the notes column. Questions must be answered and assumptions verified before the estimate is complete. I also used the notes column for any uncovered solutions, helpful libraries, or research findings.

- To arrive at an estimate, I averaged the low and high task estimates, then added 20% as a "fudge factor" for everything I forgot.

- If I wanted the number of calendar days, useful for committing to a ship date, I divided the total hours estimated by the ideal hours per day.

Table 5-1. Task estimation

Task	Low Estimate	High Estimate	Notes, Questions
Build out the login page	4	8	Use devise gem

There are many other estimation techniques out there. My method is based on personal experience rather than research. It is lightweight but ignores individual variation and team dynamics. If you want to learn estimation in depth, I'd recommend *Software Estimation: Demystifying the Black Art* by Steve McConnell. The Agile methodology has its own way of tracking the future speed of software development as well.

Getting feedback on how your estimates track with reality improves the process. While you get coarse feedback on the accuracy of your estimates when you hit or miss your ship dates, tracking task time helps you see what sections of your estimate are incorrect. This is tedious, however. Tracking forgotten yet required tasks is also helpful. If you or your team omitted a required activity from the project task list, think about how to make sure that doesn't happen in the future.

If a project is big, break estimates into milestones. This allows for more frequent check-ins and reports. These are helpful for letting a client or other teams understand progress. If a task takes longer than you think, you may need to course correct. This typically involves sacrificing scope or pushing a delivery date.

When a task is taking longer than you estimated, you *must* tell people who are depending on the completion of that task. If you have thought of a way to deliver the functionality on time using a different solution, share that. But even if you haven't, what everyone wants to avoid is a nasty surprise toward the end of a project. No one likes that.

There are some situations which don't require estimation. Part of the joy of a side project is that you can explore new technologies and techniques without commiting to a timeline. Unless, that is, you are trying to work on your planning skills, in which case, estimate away. Work you do for free, such as open source work, also requires less planning and estimation. However, if you have users of your software, they'll welcome a road map.

Others rely on your work. Estimating delivery allows them to plan.

Sincerely,

Dan

Debug systems

Dear new developer,

Being able to fix a problem in a system, especially when you don't understand everything, is a valuable skill to practice. Here are a few thoughts about this process:

- Make the problem as simple as possible. Start with the reported issue. Keep isolating and removing pieces to see if the problem persists. Modern systems are complex, and the less you must think about, the better.

- Begin with a hypothesis and work to prove it, refining it as you know more information. Sometimes I find it helpful to write the hypothesis down as that in itself can expose areas for investigation.

- Determine the desired end state. Fixing the root of the problem is usually the best course of action. There may be times when that is too costly, and fixing the symptoms or providing a workaround is what is needed.

- Pay attention if anything seems amiss or strange, no matter how small. These are clues.

- Keep notes about what you've tried. Put them in a chat system if the debugging is high priority or if you want to collaborate with others, say on fixing a production system during an outage. Or take notes in a local text file if it is a bug you're trying to understand in your local environment.

- If the bug is new, examine recent changes to the system. These are not always the cause, but often are part of the problem. Rarely does a system degrade spontaneously.

- Write an automated test which shows the faulty behavior. This will speed up your fix because it gives you a tight loop of "run test, make change, run test, make change." Having a test ensures your changes fix the bug. Adding this test to a suite will prevent this bug from popping up again.

- Follow the flow of data. Start at user input or data storage when isolating the issue. See where it first appears. For example, in a three-tier web application, start with either the browser or the relational database.

- Minimize impact to users. If you are working on a production bug, ideally you can test on staging. This gives you the most flexibility. If you must debug on production, limit debugging statements to certain users or in hidden comments.

- Make sure that where you are testing mirrors as closely as possible the system where the bug appears. Otherwise, you will spend time chasing environment differences—data or traffic are especially difficult to replicate.

Let's get a bit more concrete. One time I helped a friend debug a system for his client. The client was seeing doubled orders on his ecommerce site. That is, someone would order five widgets on the site, but the system recorded two orders, resulting in ten widgets shipped. It didn't happen with every order placed. There was no discernible pattern. There were no recent changes to the code of the ordering subsystem—it was a PHP application, and I was able to verify that by looking at file timestamps.

No one was happy. The customers weren't happy about being charged twice. The client wasn't happy about shipping product twice. My friend wasn't happy because his client was unhappy. He had examined the system and didn't have any luck finding the issue.

I had never worked with this ecommerce package before nor any like it. There was no staging environment. I was debugging in the dark. I didn't even have a way to submit test orders—any order I put in would result in my credit card being charged.

What I had was database and server access. I also had a list of the customers who had been double charged. My hypothesis was that something in the code was causing this behavior only for these specific customers, so I set out to find out what they had in common.

After a brief look at the PHP code, I realized that understanding the codebase would take a long time. So I started by looking at the web server log files with grep, vi, and all the other great Unix tools, seeking anything amiss. I noticed something weird. The logs showed the server was restarted often: every 15 minutes. After further investigation, the restart times lined up with the double charges.

I looked at the cron settings and found that someone had added a line that restarted the web server regularly. I asked my friend and the client if they knew why; no one did. I disabled the cron job that restarted the server. We watched for a week to see if the double orders continued.

They did not. Success!

For this client, fixing the symptom was enough due to a planned move to another ecommerce package. I didn't need to dive in and try to fix the root cause.

Debugging modern systems means working across many pieces of software, some of which you may be unfamiliar with. Being able to hypothesize, test small changes, and notice things that don't seem quite right are all parts of successful debugging.

Sincerely,

Dan

Assume positive intent

Rick Manelius is an MIT engineer turned web developer turned startup CXO (operations, product, and technology). You can connect and learn more at https:// rickmanelius.com/LND.

Dear new developer,

Chris could have become my worst nightmare. He was a key stakeholder and decision maker on the largest active account that my company was dependent upon for its financial stability. That wasn't the problem. The issue was that we were midway through the initial project deliverables and it was becoming apparent to team members on both sides that the budget specified on the contract was insufficient to deliver a solution that would actually meet the needs of their business. This was a huge problem. I was doing my best to navigate the situation and keep calm on the outside, but on the inside, I was stressed to the max knowing that it was possible that we could lose the account and suffer a significant financial loss.

As time went on, tensions continued to rise. Additional meetings were scheduled to discuss budgets and contracts. People started to become irritable, dig in their heels, and act in ways that were clear signs of CYA (cover your ass) in progress.

Chris could have crushed me, and yet he didn't. In fact, he did the exact opposite and taught me an incredibly valuable lesson. Amid the bickering on one phone call, he asked his colleagues to stop this behavior and to assume positive intent instead. He went on to describe how this is a philosophy he'd adopted in his personal and professional life as a means of being more efficient, effective, and solution focused. After all, approaching any situation with the opposite mindset results in wasted time and energy. Assuming negative intent means you're spending lots of time second-guessing everyone's motivations, being combative instead of collaborative, and slowing everything down by having to update contracts meticulously instead of going off of a handshake.

What about when...?

No, I wouldn't recommend applying this advice universally and haphazardly. Here are a few caveats:

- It's 100% reasonable to have a high degree of skepticism within a low-trust environment. For example, I would never assume positive intent and allow my daughter to be alone with a registered sex offender just because the person claimed they had changed. I would also never trust an alcoholic with a house full of liquor. Once a person has violated trust against a particular metric, it's okay to take a different position in order not to put yourself in harm's way.

- This advice is not without risk. Some people will leverage this against you. There are con artists and sociopaths out there. Martha Stout claims 4% of the population falls into this category. In short, if you start from a place of positive intent, you are going to get screwed over by at least 1 out of every 25 people you encounter because they literally have no moral compass. However, in my experience, the rewards outweigh the risks. To invert the statistic by Martha, 24 out of 25 people can feel legitimately bad if they know they've caused harm to someone else. Essentially, the vast majority of the population has a conscience that acts as the moral compass to steer them from intentionally causing harm to others. It doesn't always work, but it's better than nothing. And given that 96% of people fall into this category, I feel there is a greater risk in approaching those relationships from a place of distrust.

The ROI of trust

There is an entire book called *The Speed of Trust* that provides qualitative and quantitative evidence that high trust situations result in massive gains in efficiency and effectiveness in relationships. We know this intuitively. If we are skeptical of an expensive new product or service, we might spend hours of time researching to make sure we're making the right decision. However, if we get a recommendation from someone we trust, that may be all we need to decide in an instant.

So if trust is so valuable, how can we get there more quickly? Well, there are two different ways. We can start from a place of skepticism until someone has proven themselves worthy to be trusted. Or we can start from a place of positive intent right from the beginning and keep it there until they violate that trust. Both are feasible, but only by extending trust first will most relationships ever get to the place where you can experience the gains outlined in Stephen M. R. Covey's book.

Just remember there are caveats. It's all a matter of whether you're willing to accept the risks!

—Rick

Express gratitude

Dear new developer,

Being grateful makes me happier. It works for others too—two researchers from the University of California found that when they asked people to write about what they were grateful for, after ten weeks, they felt better about their lives.[2]

---

[2]www.health.harvard.edu/healthbeat/giving-thanks-can-make-you-happier

When I am frustrated with a colleague, a poorly documented technology, or code that isn't behaving, taking a step back and being thankful helps. Software development is an awesome career, because:

- Engineers are usually treated well.

- It is lucrative.

- There is a relatively low barrier to entry.

- Challenges are varied.

- It is a broad industry with many different domains to work in.

- Many jobs allow autonomy.

- Remote work is a possibility.

- Continuous learning is welcomed.

- Developers are in high demand.

When I think about these benefits, it makes the frustrations easier to bear.

It's also important to express gratitude toward others. Every project is a group effort. Thanking team members builds rapport and makes any future difficult conversations easier.

When expressing gratitude, don't be obsequious. You don't need to overthank team members. A simple "thank you" will work wonders. When saying thanks:

- Be professional. Make it short and sweet.

- Be specific: "thanks for pairing with me and debugging the XYZ component yesterday" is better than "thanks for your help."

- Spread it around. Include your peers and people from other departments.

Being grateful makes me a better teammate. Who would you rather work with? A sullen, unhappy, grumpy coworker or one who regularly shows appreciation?

Sincerely,

Dan

Cultivate the skill of undivided attention

Josh Thompson *looks forward to being a senior developer someday. He's only a few years into his career in the software development industry but enjoys getting to bring knowledge and skills from his prior careers into his current role. He lives in (and works remotely from) Golden, CO, with his wife and loves to rock climb and read books and can often be spotted in Denver area climbing gyms or local crags.*

Dear new developer,

You *know* that there's a chasm between your skill level and that of the mythical "senior software developer."

If you build a list of topics you encounter on your job that, if learned to a deep enough level, would put you on the same level as a senior developer, you'll end up even more demoralized than before compiling that list.

No need to assemble this list yourself! I've done it for you.

Here's the list of topics that I'd need to dedicate significant time to, in order to close the gap between me and the senior developers on our team, that I've encountered in my last two days of work:

- Breaking complex unknowns into simpler unknowns that can be further split into individual tickets

- Adding tests to complex, legacy code to guide further refactoring of said code

- Using `grep` to comb through server logs to diagnose a hard-to-identify-and-reproduce problem

- Provisioning new servers

- Building bash scripts to automate complex workflows

- Digging into gem source code to shed gem dependencies while maintaining certain features

- Understanding indexing well enough to see that certain queries that we thought were using indexes were not and fix this oversight on the fly, without causing any blips in availability

Each of these line items has many books written about the topic.

It seems like you could fill a bookshelf with books that address knowledge senior developers have available to them inside their own heads.

It takes me long enough to work through a single book, so imagining a bookshelf of extracurricular reading is quite daunting.

It might feel daunting for you, too.

Leading vs. lagging indicators

The preceding list of skills is a lagging indicator of the underlying knowledge. We should not target improving lagging indicators, we should improve leading indicators.

Josh, what is this "lagging and leading indicator" stuff?

Great question!

A lagging indicator is "evidence that something has already happened."

If you got an A on a test, that is evidence that you learned the material.

A leading indicator is "evidence that something will likely happen."

If you want to get an A on a test, you should study in a similar way as others who have gotten an A on that test. Maybe you need ten high-quality hours of study to get an A, so "number of high-quality study hours" would be a leading indicator of your grade.

We no longer take tests (phew, I hated taking tests), but we get mini-tests of our knowledge, daily. We're paid to solve problems, which often require learning new things.

Rather than focusing on a list of things other developers have learned, and targeting that list, I humbly propose that a leading indicator of acquiring this kind of knowledge is "hours per week spent in a state of intentional deep work."

The preceding list of topics is a lagging indicator of a high degree of technical knowledge. Someone acquires the knowledge, and then, and only then, can demonstrate that they have it.

Leading indicators are "predictive," in that if you can identify correctly those indicators, you can predict the outcome of the issue at hand.

In this case, the issue at hand is "become significantly more experienced in the domain of software development."

I propose that a *leading indicator* of someone gaining these skills is the amount of time they spend in a state of deep work.

I'd encourage you to read *Deep Work: Rules for Focused Success in a Distracted World* by Cal Newport. The author makes a case for deep work being a key role in the success of "knowledge workers" (which includes many types of work, including, of course, software development).

If you'd rather not read the book, here's the gist, from a summary of the book:

- In order to produce the absolute best stuff you're capable of, you need to commit to deep work.

- The ability to quickly master hard things and the ability to produce at an elite level, in terms of both quality and speed, are two core abilities for thriving in today's economy.

- "To learn hard things quickly, you must focus intensely without distraction."

- "Your work is craft, and if you hone your ability and apply it with respect and care, then like the skilled wheelwright you can generate meaning in the daily efforts of your professional life."

- "The key to developing a deep work habit is to move beyond good intentions and add routines and rituals to your working life designed to minimize the amount of your limited willpower necessary to transition into and maintain a state of unbroken concentration."

Imagine two equally knowledgeable early-career software developers. They have the exact same skills on January 1. If the first software developer spends 4 hours a week doing deep work, while the second software developer spends 15 hours a week doing deep work, their trajectories will be quite different, and that second developer will quickly gain technical knowledge and proficiencies.

So, if you're an early-career software developer, track the time you spend doing deep work. That has you focusing on a leading indicator of growing in your skills.

At that point, you'll benefit from Peter Drucker's assessment:

What is measured, improves.

You'll track how many hours you spend doing deep work, and by tracking it, you'll do more and more of it.

In conclusion

Do more deep work, and over a year or two years, your skills will grow much faster than those doing less deep work. Eventually, you might find that you're doing the work of a senior developer!

Good luck!

—Josh

Build empathy

Dear new developer,

You're probably frustrated and confused. You're learning a lot and you don't understand everything. Sometimes concepts click and it all makes sense, and other times you're confused and staring at a brick wall. Perhaps you just want to make things work. But they don't.

Good.

I say that not because I'm a sadist or dislike you. I imagine you're a pretty nice person! I say that because I hope you'll remember the frustration you are experiencing. It will make you a better developer.

Why?

Because that confusion, that frustration, that dissatisfaction—it is what many users of software applications feel all the time. I've watched family members try to do tasks I'd consider simple and have seen this firsthand. People are trying to use software to help complete a task and get on with their life. The program is just a tool.

As a developer, that means:

- They don't care about the elegance of your code.

- They don't care how much you love to develop.

- They don't care if you are learning and growing.

They want to finish their job, complete their task, and check that box.

And, honestly, the tools we software developers provide are frustrating. They're buggy. They're slow. The fact that anyone from 1980 would be amazed that there's a free authoritative online encyclopedia providing answers to almost any factual question from your phone or that shopping from the couch is normal is beside the point. People are still banging their heads against the limitations and flaws of the software we provide.

I don't write this to cause you despair, new developer. Progress happens, but it happens one person at a time. Every software engineer must act with empathy toward their frustrated users. Talk to them. Understand them. *Care* about them.

If you remember the frustration you are currently feeling as you struggle to learn new technology and check your own boxes, you'll have more empathy for your users, just trying to use your product to get something done.

Sincerely,

Dan

Don't complain about the code

Dear new developer,

There will come a time when you are examining a software system and trying to understand the choices behind it. You may be looking at a class, a subsystem, or something larger, like an application's architecture.

I remember looking at a system which generated custom quotes for an industrial tool. I was modifying the software. Someone mentioned that they rebooted the server every night because of a memory leak which otherwise would bring the system down. "How janky" I thought to myself. Later I found that the team had spent significant resources debugging this problem and simply couldn't find the solution. The restart dealt with the symptoms and was the least bad option.

I promise you, at some point in your career, you'll wonder what the hell the original programmer was thinking. You'll wonder why this system is still in production. You'll wonder why someone didn't fix this. You will be tempted to trash talk this piece of software to your colleagues.

Don't do this. Why not?

- *It's not helpful*—It's perfectly acceptable to point out issues and ask questions about why choices were made. It's a good idea to suggest improvements, whether software changes, code removal, or library upgrades. But complaining about the existing system doesn't do any of that.

- *It displays a lack of empathy*—Chances are you don't know the constraints and pressures the original developer and past maintainers faced. Making judgments based on the end result without understanding the process is like hiring someone based on the color of their shirt—sure, you know something, but you certainly don't have all the information.

Trust me, new developer, in the future you'll face constraints too. Constraints like ignorance, short deadlines, or small budgets. You will make suboptimal choices. At least once in my career I've come across a boneheaded piece of code. Cursing under my breath, I wondered "who wrote this crap?" As I pulled up the commit log, my face fell as I realized that I had. Doh!

What should you do if the system doesn't work at all? In that case, understanding how this system was built is even more important—you want to prevent those issues from recurring. But again, complaining doesn't help understanding.

Sincerely,

Dan

Avoid jargon

Dear new developer,

One thing I've learned is that if you can't explain a technology choice in a way that a nonengineer can understand, you don't get it either.

It is easy to use jargon to blur your lack of understanding. Now, jargon in and of itself is not a bad thing. It's shorthand for complicated concepts. If I say "RDBMS" to another experienced developer, they'll know I refer to a piece of software which provides safe, durable, transactional data storage. See how jargon builds on itself? The word "transactional" is jargon as well.

But just as if on a car trip you take one shortcut after another, you're likely to get lost, similarly too much jargon can blind you, or at least put you in a fog.

Don't take the jargon shortcut until you have done the full drive and truly understand what you're referring to. Practice describing what you do in a way that is understandable to a layperson. An example description of an application I've worked on is "we pull real estate information from different sources and publish it." I confess, I had to rewrite that sentence a few times because I started out with jargon.

Does this mean you need to understand everything from CSS to the voltage of your power supply before you can be effective? No. What it means is that you should be careful when you are using words that you may not fully fathom. A great way to better understand them is to break them down into terms a nontechnical user might use.

As you grow in your career, you'll spend more time around people who are not engineers. These folks often make decisions which affect you, the business, and software priorities. They don't always understand how software is built. If you can explain technical concepts well, you'll be at the table when decisions are made. By avoiding jargon, or at least understanding what it means, you gain:

- Clarity for yourself
- The ability to teach others
- Influence in your organization

What's not to like?

Sincerely,

Dan

Realize time is money

Dear new developer,

Don't be penny-wise, pound-foolish. Your time is worth a lot. Spend money to achieve your goals.

I heard a client say once that their time was essentially free—they were helping rework a system and were interested in paying us, their development team, as little as possible. I understood the sentiment. As a developer, I've been overly cash conscious myself—some might even call me cheap.

However, buying services provided by someone else essentially gives you more time. Who wouldn't want another couple of hours a day?

Here are some ways to spend money that have saved me or colleagues time:

- *Buying a book or video course instead of reading free documentation*—One time, for a consulting gig, I needed to integrate with Stripe, a payment processor. I found a $30 technical ebook that illustrated, with code, the exact integration needed: taking a credit card payment from a Ruby on Rails web application. The free alternative would have been a couple of hours reading the docs and experimenting. The time I saved was worth far more than $30.

- *Buying and using tools*—I have colleagues who use commercial IDEs like JetBrains. Buying and mastering this IDE increased their software development speed.

- *Paying for support*—If your business relies on other software services, pay for support. Depending on the provider and the plan, you may receive answers to your questions more quickly or have access to experts. AWS, a cloud provider, has a support plan which gets you direct access to experienced architects. Don't hesitate to access this support, either. I had a colleague who saw corrupted images in a web application. He spent a lot of time looking at our code, but the issue was caused by the service provider. We only found that out by opening a ticket with them.

- *Buy commercial software*—Pay for a solution which meets your needs. I always ask: "is this core to the business" and "what would happen if this paid service went away" when considering options. If it is not core or is easily replaceable with another provider, buy it. You can spend a lot of time and energy splicing together "free" solutions, to say nothing of maintaining them.

- *Paying for consulting or training*—A day with a consultant can save you weeks or months of time. You are paying for their experience as well as the knowledge of their mistakes so you can avoid them.

Not all of these necessarily apply to you right now, new developer. You may have no budget to spend at work. But you can still trade money for time when it comes to learning. Get that subscription to Udemy or Safari. Buy that book. Explore that commercial tool.

Your time is precious. Don't waste it; spend money.

Sincerely,

Dan

Say no

Dear new developer,

There's an art to saying no. And there's power in doing so.

I once worked on a project creating a Yahoo clone. The lead developer fell ill and the team needed someone to step up. I said "yes, I can help." I jumped in and led the project to success. I ended up working 96 hours one week. The site launched. My company expressed their gratitude with a gift: a t-shirt and six-pack of beer.

I have learned since then how to say no.

The art is in saying no without being a jerk. You want to be a team player so flip the script and say "yes, but."

- "Yes, I'm happy to shift to working on task B, but should I finish task A first?"

- "Yes, I can help you with the release, but Jane is waiting on this feature. Should I let her know?"

- "Yes, I'd love to work on that project, but shouldn't I finish up this component first?"

Using this turn of phrase makes it clear that you are happy to help but are aware of your other obligations. Practice this with smaller requests first. Always ask for prioritization. Especially as a new developer, you often don't have the bigger picture. Maybe task B is blocking three other developers from making forward progress. Maybe that release is more important because it includes a high-priority bug fix. Maybe that component can be put on hold for now.

I have never once been dinged when I asked for prioritization. It shows that you want to work on important things, have an awareness of the bigger picture, and are flexible and helpful. Just a warning—you will be asked to estimate task completion time as soon as you ask for prioritization.

The power of saying no is that it protects your time. You only have one life to live. When you have a salaried job, there's not much downside for your company to take more of your time. Even if your boss is nice, you are responsible for establishing and protecting your boundaries. If you say "yes" all the time, you will end up working a lot of extra hours. Other aspects of your life will suffer as a result.

I enjoy working. When I was starting out, I was proud when I stayed late: "look, I'm getting stuff done" and "I'm building cool software that helps people." But the point of life is to live, not just to work. As I look back over my career, I'm proud of what I and others have built. However, a lot of that software is no more. Will I ever get any of that 96-hour work week back?

Make it clear that you're happy to help, but don't let work suck you in. Say no.

Sincerely,

Dan

Play a lot more

*During the day, **Zach Turner** is a software engineer at Culture Foundry, a full-service digital agency. At night he is a maker of things useful, useless, and everywhere in between.*

Dear new developer,

Don't forget to play. I spent the year after undergraduate working and learning. My goal was to find a job at a company, and eventually I succeeded. However, my passion dwindled because it was always put second to finding a salaried position. As a result, my desire to play with and learn about new technologies simply because they are interesting has dwindled, and my enjoyment of my job has suffered.

Allow yourself to approach the world as a kid again. Buy an electronics kit and only do the first example experiment. Learn Hello World in 30 different languages. Start a passion project without worrying about finishing it. If you do finish it, try rewriting it in a new language. Think about a tool (software) that you would like to use, no matter how small or silly, and make it. There is so much pressure to know the newest and most popular languages and frameworks and have a clean GitHub repo full of complete, relevant, and useful projects. That is especially appealing if you're looking for a job. Yes, you should have a couple projects that are showcase worthy and speak to your desire to competently code. You should also be able to speak to your desire to learn and solve problems.

At the end of the day, code is just a tool. No one faults a carpenter for having multiple hammers. I mean have you ever seen the garage of carpenter or maker; they are usually a glorious mess of projects in various states. Play and don't fear clutter. Clean as you go and organize if you must. I'd rather have the GitHub of Doc Brown over Patrick Bateman any day. You can be a competent, intelligent adult and still play. If you don't want work to become a chore, you must play.

From,

Zach Turner

Build on your own

Dear new developer,

Having a side project makes you a better developer. This is kind of a bummer, because when I get home from a day at the office, I don't want to sit in front of the computer any longer. But if you can make it happen, even if only an hour a week, you'll learn from building on your own.

Why? Because a side project lets you perform all the activities which go into a software product. You get to make all the decisions. Design, product, hosting, languages, frameworks—it's all on you. If you had a deadline, this would be a burden. When you don't, this is a learning gold mine.

Start by finding a problem you want to solve. For me, this is usually a database-driven web application, but what is important is that you are interested in applying the technology you choose to your problem. Think of a side project like taking up a new hobby that happens to involve code—a bit like a professional musician going to a jam session, but with screens and keyboards.

If you don't have an idea for a side project, but have time and interest, find an outside project you can help. Ask around at meetups or check out organizations like Code for America.

If you do code, don't feel you must make your project public. Potential employers may use it to evaluate you without your knowledge. If you make the code public, document its current state, especially if it is unfinished. This will make it clear to potential employers if a project is a work in progress.

If you don't want to write code, write prose. A blog will let you explore new technologies or business domains. Writing familiarizes you with the community, helps you understand the use cases for a technology, and can establish you as an expert.

Don't be afraid to let the side project go. I let go of a website directory I built. It was painful, but I didn't have time for it. If you aren't enjoying the project or don't have time for it, let it go. An initial commitment of six months helps me get "over the hump" that I encounter starting anything. It also helps me avoid beginning too many projects—if I can't commit for six months, I shouldn't start it. If you've been building on your own for at least that long and you find yourself avoiding it, give yourself a month off. If that time away doesn't spark renewed enthusiasm, let it go. If you have end users, make sure they can get their data. If it's an open source project, find another maintainer or mark the project as clearly in hibernation. If it's a blog, write a goodbye post.

Should you mention what you've built in interviews? Sure, like anything else, a side project is fair game to mention in an interview if it illustrates a skill relevant to the job. For instance, if you prioritize features for your side project by talking to users, that displays communication skills and user empathy.

What if you don't have time to do a side project? That's okay too. Building something outside of work is one way to get better at your craft, but certainly not the only way.

Sincerely,

Dan

Consistency is key

Dear new developer,

Sometimes you just have to grind.

It's easy to find yourself beaten up. Development, while not physically difficult, can be mentally and emotionally taxing. You can really screw things up. You write software under pressure. Even when you're part of a team, often you're working on a task into which you alone have insight. No one else knows the problem as well. Asking for help will net you advice, but not necessarily a definitive answer. Deadlines loom. You're learning on the job—figuring things out. There's always a new technology stack or framework or language or technique or term to learn.

Phew.

It can be tough—not digging ditches tough but difficult nonetheless. It's easy to get discouraged—to think you aren't making progress. But showing up is progress. I was talking to another senior developer, and we agreed that there is so much knowledge you gain only with time:

- How to navigate the command line in the most efficient way possible

- How to read a regular expression

- When to ask a question and when to keep pushing forward on the current problem

- How to ask for a raise

- How to search the Web

- How to scan logs

- How to stay calm in a crisis

This knowledge can't be taught; it must be learned. You learn it by showing up every day.

This is true of any skill you want to gain. Do you want to be good at design? Writing? Public speaking? Find a way to practice every day or every week. Six months is the minimum commitment. It's not too long, yet you'll be more than a beginner at the end. You'll have the context to know if you want to continue. Consistency of this sort has opportunity cost, however. Committing to writing a blog post every week means you'll have less time to watch your favorite TV show.

I find it scary to commit sometimes. What if I choose the wrong technology? What if I don't like writing a blog? The good news is I can stop. Especially early in your career, you can take a mulligan easily—you're being hired for potential rather than skill set.

When I'm aiming for consistency, I like a paper calendar to track my efforts. I put a big fat "X" on it every day I show up. Getting to put that "X" on the calendar motivates me. It has even forced me to get up out of bed at night, just to keep a streak going.

Consistency gives you a chance to improve and permission to fail. If you are working on problems that are hard for you every day, you won't hit a home run every time. Heck, you can't expect to always hit a single. But if you can show up and put in the hard work, you'll improve. If you write a blog post every day for a year, some will be good, some will be bad, and some will be horrible. But if 10% of them are good, that's three times more useful content than regular good monthly blog posts.

Keep it up. Good things will happen.

Sincerely,

Dan

In conclusion

Practices help you improve a facet of the software craft. Whether reading code, empathizing with the users of your software, or communicating with nontechnical colleagues, these techniques don't always come naturally.

You must practice them repeatedly, but when you do, they will get easier. You will begin to perform them intuitively. They'll become habits, and then second nature.

Understanding the Business

Software does not exist in a vacuum. It is written for and by people. Sometimes software is created just for fun or to satisfy the needs of the creator. Other times, the software exists to serve a business. Employees of a company think that a software product can be sold or need custom software built to enable other employees to perform a task more efficiently.

In this chapter, I'll discuss what you should know about the employer who buys your labor. I'll talk about "businesses" or "companies," but these lessons all apply to other organizations such as universities or nonprofits. Within any organization, there are constraints and invisible structures not immediately obvious. These include:

- *The profit motive*—Businesses want to make money and need to provide value for customers.

- *What business the company is in*—Businesses that sell to restaurants have different constraints than those which sell to banks.

- *The type of customers the business serves*—Selling to CTOs is different from selling to consumers.

© Dan Moore 2020
D. Moore, *Letters to a New Developer*, https://doi.org/10.1007/978-1-4842-6074-6_6

- *The employees*—Businesses are made up of people who are often concerned with the preservation of their livelihoods.

- *The origins of the business*—The founding goals of the organization impact decisions and culture.

- *Past decisions and history*—Objectives added to the company's goals after founding based on interactions with customers, employees, and other stakeholders.

Understanding the goals and methods of businesses will help you write better software. By learning more about the business beyond the engineering team, you'll make better choices. When you are hands-on-keyboard writing code, you might name variables in a more comprehensible way or deliver a project more quickly by purchasing a service rather than building it. You'll also understand why other employees may not be excited about yet another application to learn.

Learning more about how a business runs makes you a more integral part of the company.

Software is about people, not code

Dear new developer,

Your code is a means to an end: delivering value to the business paying you.

When I was a new developer, I thought that software development was all about code. After all, code was most of what I worked on.

Sure, there were other tasks that mattered:

- How to interface with existing systems and components

- What the problem being solved was

- How to deliver it

- How to ensure it met the specifications

- How it would be maintained and operated

But the writing of code felt like the most important part of my job. It was the most tangible and fundamental. After all, if the software doesn't exist, all those other tasks won't matter, right?

This led me to focus on how to best write code. Among other activities, I:

- Wrote up a style guide for the company

- Learned how to decompile java bytecode to reverse engineer proprietary software (shh, don't tell anyone)

- Researched new technologies
- Read and commented in online forums about software craftsmanship
- Argued about code formatting
- Joined a design pattern discussion group
- Attended meetups and blogged about my opinions and findings

I wanted to be better at writing code; I thought this was the same thing as getting better at developing software.

However, I soon learned that people were more relevant than code to the overall success of a software project. I saw interesting codebases abandoned for lack of a market or other business flaws. For example, I joined a startup building an application which let people browse real estate data on their phone—in 2004, when the user experience of phone apps was miserable. No matter how good the software was, a poor deployment environment doomed the codebase.

I'd assumed the code was the critical piece of software development. But really, the people, developers, other teams, and end users, were far more important because:

- Software is created for people and their purposes. It doesn't exist on its own, isolated from human needs.
- People have choices about the software they use. Even for applications with no competition, such as internal business apps, users need to be heard to buy in.
- Most people don't know or care about the code. They're just trying to get something done. The most beautiful, well-tested, flexible, configurable, documented, future-proofed codebase that does the wrong thing is useless.

At the end of the day, code is a general-purpose tool, like accounting or legal contracts. Lovely software isn't an end in itself. Instead, software must solve real-world problems of real people.

Sincerely,

Dan

Outcomes over output

Mark Sawers has been practicing software engineering for almost 25 years, as a developer, architect, and manager.

Dear new developer,

As a software engineer, it's easy to take our eye off the ball. The ball we really want to pay attention to isn't the stuff we focused on in college. The ball is improving business/organizational outcomes. There isn't a course of study or advanced degree on this, because it's bespoke and custom to every organization.

You are on a team in your organization's grand game to help the underserved, make money for shareholders, find some cure, save the planet, or whatever its mission. A software-intensive system improves information access, automates tasks, entertains, and so on. You pair with your business discipline in conceiving, building, testing, and operating systems that advance the game.

Your real value to your organization is in improving outcomes—not *directly* in how well you wield language X, tool Y, or process Z, and not in how many features you add in a sprint, how many bugs you fix in one day, how much code you reviewed yesterday, how many answers you posted in Slack, how many documents you wrote last month, and so on. Those are just a means to an end.

Yes, we need to constantly develop and hone technical skills (analysis, modeling, diagramming, programming, unit testing, etc.) and tool knowledge (languages, frameworks, utilities, operating systems, etc.), but don't mistake this for the endgame.

Yes, we should measure productivity; we do care about efficiency and throughput. But more product features, the latest tech, continuous deployment, two-factor authentication, and so on are not the goal. More is usually less, in my experience as a user. Isn't that yours as well?

The goal is not output; the goal is *outcome*. The outcome is more revenue, more profit, more users, more product availability, happier users ... right?

So, wait, isn't that someone else's job? What do you know about forecasting and measuring profit, anticipating user needs? Isn't that on the product owner? The product manager? Marketing? And isn't uptime the operations team's responsibility? And finding problems the QA team's responsibility?

You are on a multidisciplinary team. You have at least one vital role to play on this team. Engineering is your trained discipline, and likely you focused purely on development. The smaller the company/business unit, the more hats you will wear. Yes, your main contribution is technical, but in service of the bottom line. *Don't stay in your lane!* Different perspectives are essential to this game.

Your product owner doesn't have a patent on designing end-user features. And they may not be thinking about measuring success. Help them define the metrics and build those collection and reporting tools into the product. After you deploy a new feature, assess its success; don't immediately move on to the next feature.

Okay, so do I eat my own dog food? I try. The tech side requires lots of cognitive space, and so outcomes are easily short-shafted. Also, I have found this holistic perspective difficult to practice in large organizations. There is a lot of specialization. It fragments responsibility. Incentives are set along discipline silos. My suggestion is to play your organization's games (don't leave that bonus on the table!) but bring your enlightened perspective as best as you can.

Good luck,

Mark

Business process crystallization

Dear new developer,

Software freezes business processes and makes them less flexible. This influences how nontechnical team members think about software and developers.

What's a business process? These are the series of steps and interactions which are "how things get done" in an organization.

For instance, let's consider the business process of selling custom software, as you might if you worked as a freelancer.

If I have an application to write, the process might go a bit like this:

- Document the requirements.
- Have the client sign off on them.
- Design the program.
- Code the application.
- Test it.
- Deploy the system.
- Handle any changes that the client wants.

This is a fluid business process. If I learn I need additional requirements or have questions after I have started coding, I send an email and ask.

There are also constraints on this process, which dictate what can be accomplished when. For example, client sign-off blocks subsequent steps—I won't move forward without it. Not all steps of a process need to be completed, either. If I can't write COBOL, but the application is written in that language, the above process will not be completed, at least not by me. I won't be deploying a code change if I can't make it. All parties to this business process work within those constraints.

The goal of using software to automate business processes is to make them faster or cheaper. For example, using mail merge saves time when printing out form letters. Automating processes with software has costs, however. Mistakes happen faster as well. People's ability to handle ambiguity and make human decisions is removed from the process. Processes also become more difficult to change. Instead of changing a document or checklist, a developer must be involved.

So, what happens when a business process should change but has been encoded in software? People are more flexible than computers, so they adjust to the automated process, even if it is partially or completely obsolete. It may force employees to take extra steps or use workarounds. However, if it isn't worth the investment to change, the software "solution" remains, clogging up the business processes it was meant to assist.

Software can handle vast amounts of data with few errors at superhuman speeds. But it also crystallizes business processes, making change harder. If, like me, you think software is the solution to most business problems, realize that nonengineers understand the downsides and are justifiably wary of software panaceas.

Sincerely,

Dan

Businesses spend money to make money

Dear new developer,

Businesses usually spend money to make money. This is why a business hires you, why it rents that shiny new office building, and why it spends money on tools to help you do your job. It is even why business pays severance. It's sometimes cheaper to pay employees to leave than to keep them on the payroll; in the long term, the company will make more money by paying people to leave now. In all these cases, the organization writes checks because someone, somewhere, believes that doing so will help the company make more money. Even if you don't have a voice in any spending decisions, this fact illuminates how and why such decisions are made.

Unlike personal spending, which is rarely an investment that offers a return, business spending is about finding leverage to increase profits. But such spending is always uncertain. If a return was guaranteed, others would notice, step in, and bid up the price of the opportunity. For example, if a business could spend $100 on search engine ads and acquire a new customer worth $110, the company would buy those ads all day long. But other companies would soon bid up the cost of the ads because they'd want to acquire that customer. So taking informed but uncertain bets is part of running a business.

However, making money is not the only reason businesses spend money. Sometimes the CEO wants to burnish their public image. Inertia or unmanaged growth can lead to spending. Whether that poor cash management harms the organization depends on revenue and expenses. For instance, when you are starting up, it makes sense to watch every penny. When a business is established, spending a thousand dollars a month on cloud servers so an engineer can do their work is worthwhile.

At times, it can be hard to know if an expense will lead directly to revenue. If the company donates money to a local charity, will that spending result in valuable publicity or be ignored? No one knows.

What does this mean to you, new developer?

When you join a project or company, consider the economics. How is it going to make money? What are the assumptions? Is there a way to spend money to accelerate delivery and/or revenue? Ask team members how this effort will generate revenue. Asking these questions helps you understand why the project exists; it's no fun to work on a pointless piece of software. You'll also get a feel for the kind of bets that this organization takes, including scale, preparatory work, and target market. Finally, you'll be better equipped to make decisions on the microscale based on macro understanding.

A developer who can execute the details while understanding the big picture is more valuable than someone who can only do the former.

Sincerely,

Dan

Understand the business model

Dear new developer,

A business model is jargon for "how a company makes money in a repeatable profitable fashion." When you are an employee, your code is written to help execute against this business model. Learning about this lets you make smarter on-the-ground decisions.

To learn about the business model, ask about how your company makes money. Every organization needs revenue, even nonprofits or universities. Make sure you understand what is being sold, whether a product or a service. For large organizations, there may be multiple sources of revenue; in that case, focus on what your department provides.

If no one can explain how the business makes or will make money, then the organization is either nascent and hunting for a business model, or it is in a heap of trouble. The former presents great learning opportunities, if you can handle the risk. The latter should be avoided. Differentiate between the two by asking how many employees the organization has. While there are exceptions, as a rule of thumb, a company with more than ten employees and no business model is firmly in the "heap of trouble" category.

After you know what is being sold, ask how it is produced. Crucially, you want to know how software helps sell more of the product or produces it at a lower cost. This, new developer, is where your skills will be applied. You produce software. By knowing how the business uses it, you can understand what type of problems you'll be working on.

Identifying the domain in which the business operates also helps you understand what you need to learn. When I was employed by a real estate brokerage, I learned about that business—what is involved when a house changes owners, who owns and distributes housing data, what is the typical flow of a real estate transaction, and even what jargon is used. If your company sells GIS software, learn what GIS stands for, who buys it, and what a customer uses it for. Immerse yourself in the sales and marketing materials for your company and products.

Once you know the domain, the software you write will more directly address the problems of that domain. If problems are common, pattern match to recommend other solutions. For instance, almost every business needs customer relationship management software. An easy way to learn the domain is to create a glossary to ensure common terms are used by both business and software teams. In addition to informing you, such a glossary avoids misunderstandings when a word means different things to different organizational units.

Learn about the problems the business teams face: how do they acquire customers? How do they keep them happy? Offer software techniques to help solve these issues. For example, when I worked at that real estate company, I took a statistics course and researched machine learning libraries because we were building a home value estimation product based on our access to real estate data. The product would have helped us find new customers. Knowing the business domain and needs led me to research appropriate software techniques and technologies.

Another reason to understand how the business incorporates software you build into its revenue generation model is, frankly, a bit gruesome. When the business is under stress due to a recession, you want to be attached to a part of the business that makes money. Knowing the business model and understanding how your software is connected to it allows you to guess how likely it is that you'll be part of a cost-cutting measure—a layoff. For example, if you are part of a team building the core product, you are less likely to lose your job than if you are working on a research and development project.

Understanding the economic model of your employer will help you communicate with and thrive in a business.

Sincerely,

Dan

No company is a monolith

Dear new developer,

When I was new to the business world, I thought that companies acted rationally and with singular purpose. Boy was I wrong. Businesses are full of people with all the messiness, politics, and unpredictability of any group of humans.

I remember when an old-timer at my first job talked about empire builders. His perspective was that above a certain level in the corporate hierarchy, there's not much interest in accomplishing company goals. Instead, people want to accumulate more power—budget, headcount, influence. This causes turf wars that can be confusing to people at a lower level in the organization.

I was skeptical when he first mentioned this, but I have seen absurd behavior best explained by this desire with my own eyes. At one point in the mid-2000s, I was hired as a contractor for a relatively high rate. I showed up bright-eyed and bushy-tailed ready to work. But there was nothing to do.

I asked my contracting company what I should do. The answer was "bill 40 hours a week." I tried to ask my manager about the situation but couldn't find him—he was in meetings all day long. I asked employees on my team what to do—no one wanted to give me any tasks. To be fair, this was in the middle of an economic downturn. I never found out exactly why I was hired when there was no work for me to do, but I believe the manager was maintaining his budget and headcount. As for me, I spent a lot of time browsing the Internet. I remember browsing a dating site and having a fellow contractor advise me to at least turn my screen so it wasn't visible from the doorway. I have never felt more useless in my life and left after three months.

Above a certain size, there are factions in a company which affect how you can do your job. By the way, there are factions when an employer is under that size, but the infighting is less frequent, either because there is more cohesion or because the survival of the company is uncertain. Smaller companies have fewer places for people who aren't pulling their weight to hide. I can't give you a firm size beyond which factions begin to impact employees, but I do remember a colleague mentioning that at 60, bad apples found hiding spots.

What does this mean for you, new developer? Since companies are composed of people, the interactions between them impact hiring. You may be ignored for reasons entirely unrelated to you or your skills; perhaps the hiring manager is being transferred or losing influence.

If you are an employee, learn the various factions and players. Observe relationships and ask your boss questions, delicately, about the politics of the company. You may want to associate yourself with a faction; a rising camp seems to me to be the best, but fortunes change fast. As you observe these relationships, you'll start to gain insight into why one project might be funded and another starved.

I should mention an alternative I've chosen: avoidance. I have no patience for this kind of stuff. I'd rather find a trustworthy boss and work hard to make him or her look great. That's probably why I've spent most of my life at small companies. But if you're working in a larger organization, be aware of the existence of internal politics.

Sincerely,

Dan

Where do developers fit in?

Dear new developer,

Writing software is a portable skill set. Almost every company uses software, just like double-entry accounting, a technology invented in the 1400s. However, companies use software in different ways to build and sell their products. How software integrates into this process affects developer happiness. Here are three different types of companies that use software:

- Software product companies sell software.
- Consulting companies sell hours or developer expertise.
- Every other company sells a product other than software but uses software to run their business.

As a new software developer, knowing how software is used at your employer helps you understand the business. The larger the company, the more likely it is to span categories, however. Certain types of companies will allow you to learn new technologies. Others will provide the opportunity to gain deep business domain knowledge.

Software product companies sell software, typically to other companies—restaurants, other software companies, housing manufacturers—or to individuals: editors, task management systems, bingo card creation for teachers. As a developer in this company, you will learn the intricacies of the customer domain. For instance, I worked at a company which had a software system which prevented texting while driving. I learned about automotive data collection hardware and telco sales cycles. If successful, these companies often have a business model that allows for high margins, which can lead to good salaries and benefits. However, you may find working in the same domain for years to be boring. If established, these companies often use older technologies. Legacy systems make money.

In contrast, consulting companies, which sell developer hours, often move developers between domains. You will get a variety of experience with different business models, customers, and problems. There are often new, "green field" projects to work on which usually mean new technologies to learn. An hour worked for a client is an hour billed, so your efforts are directly related to revenue.

If you are looking to eventually start your own company, consulting businesses have low barriers to entry: no overhead and no up-front investment in building a product. You only need a laptop, an Internet connection, and someone willing to hire you. However, if this business model seems attractive, be aware that until the company attains a certain size, your revenue is tightly coupled to your time, which can make vacation hard to take.

On the other hand, as an employee of a consulting company, know there is no exit strategy for the founders and that the value of the business is often tightly coupled to their skill sets, especially if the company is small. While some consulting companies have products to sell, there is usually limited recurring revenue. This means that the business goes through cycles of growing and shrinking as client needs change. Because of this sales cycle, the company may take on less exciting projects to pay the bills, projects that you may have to work on. Many consulting companies I've been part of have tried to specialize, but few have had the cash position to turn down lucrative projects when payroll was due. Consulting projects can have tight deadlines which may lead to excessive hours.

And then there's all the rest of the companies. These companies use software. It may even be core to their business, but as an enabler, not as a revenue-generating product. Examples include service companies like real estate brokerages or vinyl banner manufacturing companies. These businesses are often stable and profitable. Software quality and process tend to be less mature, though this obviously varies. If the process quality is lower, introducing better ones will be a competitive advantage. Unlike consulting companies, you'll be immersed in the business domain and will learn it well.

However, if developers aren't directly tied to revenue generation, they won't be as highly valued—or paid. Software engineering teams can be viewed as an expense rather than an asset. If the company is small, you may be alone, limiting your capacity for growth. Leadership may not understand or care about the difficulties of software development.

Knowing how your business uses software will help you understand how they view developers. This reveals the challenges and opportunities awaiting you.

Sincerely,

Dan

Hammers

Dear new developer,

I was talking to a friend the other day about differences between small and big company life, and he used a metaphor so good I'm going to steal it.

Imagine a problem is a rock. Your employer is a hammer with which to carve said rock into a beautiful sculpture—that is to say, to solve the problem. As an employee, you can join a small nimble company, which is like a brick hammer, or a large, slower-moving organization, more like a sledgehammer.

The smaller the hammer, the easier it is to pick up, manipulate, and reorient if you need to approach the rock from a different angle. In the same way, a small company can choose different approaches to their problem and quickly rework processes.

If one, on the other hand, chooses the sledgehammer to shape the rock, there's a lot of force in each swing, but not much precision. This power makes progress easier if the initial approach is correct. But if change is required, it's more effort. The weight of the hammer makes it harder to reorient. Large companies can solve big problems but don't shift direction easily.

Certain problems are amenable to bigger hammers—anything that requires a long sales cycle, large amounts of capital, or extensive research and development. Other problems are suited to a small hammer—small markets or uncertain domains where nimble experimentation is rewarded.

The larger the business, the more leverage and power can be brought to bear. I've worked at big companies, and I can tell you they were working on problems of tremendous size and scope. However, a lot of time and effort was spent coordinating those endeavors. Process changes required navigating bureaucracy and red tape.

At a smaller company or a startup, teams I was on didn't have bandwidth to take on multiple projects. Doing more than one or at most two projects was a recipe for distraction and inefficiency. However, it was easy to try different approaches and incorporate customer feedback. This flexibility extended to my job definition as well. At a smaller company, I've been expected to perform a variety of roles and adapt to changing situations. I worked at a startup where I had two CEOs and four different jobs in eight months—with not a formal job description in sight.

Both big hammers and small hammers chisel a rock; both big companies and small organizations solve problems. The type of a company affects how they go about doing so.

Sincerely,

Dan

Starting a company

Dear new developer,

Later in your career, you may want to run your own company. I would not advise doing so as a new developer, because running a business is at least as complicated as writing software. If you are learning both at once, you're setting yourself up for a world of stress.

Eventually, if you decide that you want to build a software company, you may decide to self-fund the effort. Self-funding means you only spend money that you have saved or that the business can earn. The other path is raising funding from investors, but that's riskier in some ways. By accepting outside money, you now have to satisfy both your customers and your investors.

Here are guidelines for building a bootstrapped business:

- *It will take longer than you think*—For any meaningful value of "it," expect the process to take longer than planned. Whether acquiring your first customer, building your product, or anything else, plan for it to take longer than you imagine. Companies have processes tuned over time, and these will need to be implemented anew at your fledgling company.

- *Know your financial runway*—Know this number for both the company and yourself. Find out how much you spend each month (your "burn rate") and how much you have in the bank. Don't forget to allow a buffer for you to find a different job—typically, you won't be able to step from a cratered startup on Friday into a full-time job on Monday.

- *Extend that runway*—Lower your burn rate as much as possible. Cut back on spending. If applicable, make sure your family is on board. Because everything will take longer than you think, you want a longer runway than you think you'll need. Look for other sources of money to feed and clothe yourself. Options include:

  - Digging into savings

  - Borrowing against assets using HELOCs or similar financial instruments

  - Getting a loan from relatives

  - Selling assets

  - Consulting work, including moonlighting

  - Having a spouse with income

- *Consider your emotional runway*—However, more important than your financial runway is your emotional runway. How much emotional energy do you possess? Are you in the middle of a trying life event like a move or new baby? Or is your personal life relatively settled? Talk about the stress of possible business issues with your spouse or family. Think about other emotional difficulties you've had and how you handled them. Definitely plan for some high highs and low lows.

- *Talk to your customer*—Find your customers and learn from them. Where do they congregate online? If you don't find a place, make one and invite potential customers to join. This was one of the great assets a former cofounder brought to our startup. She had deep domain expertise and many customer connections. Right when I started, we had prospects willing to give us feedback, whether via interviews, beta testing, product advisory councils, or surveys.

- *Everything is borked all the time*—In a company which is just starting, you don't have time to do everything correctly. This can be embarrassing, but if you are providing value to customers, they will stick around. Just keep improving things. Accept a certain amount of brokenness.

- *Know your market*—As previously mentioned, talk to your customers. But don't do only that. Market research and reading will help you too. But nothing is as good as the feedback of sales. As you build your product or service, you will be surprised by what your market wants. For instance, at that startup, we thought our customers wanted a polished user experience. We were surprised when a customer said our first, grungy user interface was great.

If you do start a company, with success you'll move away from coding day to day. One of the benefits of building a company is that you can scale up and work on bigger problems. But to do so, you'll have to accept more distance from the actual writing of software. Over the years, I've seen many companies grow from founders to tens or hundreds of people. In almost every case, the founders moved toward management or a strategic role and away from the code.

Sincerely,

Dan

Learn from your customers

Dear new developer,

I love to learn from customers who buy or use the products I make. It's a great opportunity for me to interact with folks whose lives my work is improving. Well, hopefully improving—if not they'll tell me. Having direct feedback from them will help me build better software.

Now, the ways you can do this differ based on the size and type of your company. If you want feedback, ask your team how they get it now. Participating in customer support and reaching out and proactively talking to customers are great ways to get insights.

In the past, teams I have been on have used ticketing systems such as Zendesk or a common email inbox to coordinate customer support. I got an account on these systems and answered emails or closed tickets. This gave me a feel for the rough edges of the product and helped build empathy for users: "why couldn't they see that to do task XYZ, you just click here and then here and then… oh, that's why. Oh. Ohhhh."

If you do this, you will also learn the surprising ways your product or service is used. This may reveal flaws or bugs—those you can file and fix to make the experience better. Even if you aren't fixing support issues, simply reading them will give you an awareness of problematic areas of your offering. However, you will get a biased view of your customers if you only look at support tickets; very few happy customers open support requests.

For an alternative view, consider scheduling a monthly meeting with customers. Aim for 15 minutes to an hour in duration. Having this meeting lets you hear directly from them what they like about the product and, more importantly, what is missing or broken. Customers also enjoy direct access to a developer—this may be a new experience for them and can enhance customer loyalty. If you are in a meeting, take notes or, with permission, record the call. This will let you go back and review the details of the feedback when needed.

When I did this, I rotated between different customers; getting multiple viewpoints helped me triangulate. If an issue was common across multiple users, it was higher priority. Capture the feedback in a tracking system, even if you don't address the issues raised immediately. These in-person calls also let me inform customers of new or relevant features. Frankly, at times I found this meeting exhausting because of the offhanded feature requests. When combined with my engineering mindset—as soon as I hear a problem, I think "what would it take to implement that?"—I often felt overwhelmed. Try to avoid that mindset and be an open listener. Focus on the problems mentioned, not the client's proposed solutions.

If you seek out direct customer feedback, you'll deliver less code. However, you're more likely to deliver useful functionality. Don't get defensive when your product is criticized. Customers pay you money and want the product to work for them. Remember to seek out customers with a variety of perspectives. You don't want feedback only from new customers or power users.

Don't commit to anything during your interaction. It's better to have such suggestions proceed through the normal planning process. Especially as a new developer, you may not have the authority to make such commitments anyway. Check with your team to see if you can share the product road map if the customer asks.

Finally, when seeking feedback, ask the customers about their pressing problems, even if beyond the scope of your solution. In this way, you'll gain insight into problems they may have that are adjacent to your systems. This can lead to interesting new directions for your software.

Customer service requires different skills than developing software. I find it choppy. You encounter folks who are having a rough day and who might take it out on you. But customer service also makes sure that you, the person helping build the software, understand what your customers and users experience.

Sincerely,

Dan

In conclusion

As a developer, I find it easy to get wrapped up in code. After all, I like to write it. It appears to be the fundamental deliverable of software teams—no code, no value. I find software engineering, and the related disciplines of architecture and software design, mentally engaging.

However, it's worth remembering when you are slinging code for an employer that they have larger goals. Learn about the business, including domain terms, strategic objectives, and decision-making processes. Knowing how the business works allows you to write software more effectively and to lower the communication barrier between teams.

Learning

Learning is part of being a software developer. Because technology and techniques are revised and updated regularly, self-education is important for succeeding at your current position and also for future opportunities. The first half of this chapter covers abstract aspects of learning, and the second half is tactical, including specific tools I use to continue my education.

Sometimes you'll need to find a solution for a specific problem, such as how to concatenate two strings in an efficient manner. Other times what you are looking to learn might be more systemic, like how to leverage a new cloud service to save your company money.

But there are reasons to learn beyond solving the specific problems you are confronted with:

- Reading to level up your craft

- Educating yourself with theory and others' experiences to approach your work in a new way

- Picking up industry terms and concepts to enable better communication

- Mastering something new just for the joy of it

Not everyone learns the same way. I've had colleagues who loved watching videos to dig into a subject, while others find watching YouTube tedious, slow, and uninformative. Some software engineers reinforce their learning by writing down daily reflections, while others prefer hands-on tutorials.

The specific method you use to teach yourself is less important than finding a way to incorporate learning into every day of your software development career.

© Dan Moore 2020

D. Moore, *Letters to a New Developer*, https://doi.org/10.1007/978-1-4842-6074-6_7

Never stop learning

Dear new developer,

At lunch once, I asked senior engineers and managers what advice they'd give to a new developer. One answered: "never stop learning."

Like most good advice, it's simple but not easy. It's simple to remind yourself you must always be learning and improving, but I often find it difficult to carve out the time. However, trying to catch up is harder than investing time regularly and staying current.

If you are not interested in or able to learn new technologies and techniques, software development will eventually pass you by. I've seen it happen over the years. Perl used to be an in-demand programming language. Now the number of job listings mentioning Perl, a proxy of demand for the skill, are much fewer than they used to be; this indicates to me that this language is in decline.

You can still make a great living with such skills, but opportunities become fewer and fewer. You may need to move or decrease your salary expectations. There are still COBOL developers, but every year fewer companies need their services. And it's not just programming languages which regularly rise and fall in usage. The software development process has changed even in the few decades I've been working, including sea changes like extreme programming, the Agile methodology, and infrastructure as code. An example of a recent revolution is the DevOps mindset.[1]

Why do people stop learning? From observation and personal experience, I see the following reasons why people cease their education:

- *Bored*—They simply aren't interested in learning.

- *Frustrated or blocked*—They can't learn what they want to because of constraints, possibly organizational.

- *Tired*—They have too much going on, and they need their energy for other parts of their lives.

- *Comfortable*—They know what they need to know and are "punching the clock." They are doing good work now, but not improving.

- *Shifting priorities*—Other things take precedence; a new baby, health issues, or a family emergency, for example.

All of these make sense. You have a job to live your life; you don't live your life to succeed at your job.

---

[1] *Accelerate: The Science of Lean Software and DevOps: Building and Scaling High Performing Technology Organizations* is an accessible introduction to this methodology.

However, a shift in perspective, whether a new job or a new way of looking at your current position, can remove obstacles that may prevent you from learning. For example, if you are frustrated because you're a software engineer in test but you are really interested in DevOps automation, find a tool to run your tests automatically. Talk to the infrastructure team and see how you can help test their infrastructure as code deployments.

If you want to incorporate learning into your daily life, the short answer is "Google." The Internet is full of information about how to be excellent at software development.

A longer answer starts with your motivation and then proceeds toward specific tactics to execute against that goal.

- Think about why you want to learn. Is it for fun? To find a better job? To be better at your current position? To test out your theories? To solve your own problem, scratch your own itch? Because you want to make the world a better place? Finding this intrinsic motivation will help you continue when you encounter difficulties.

- From the why comes the what. What can you learn that will help you achieve your goal? Is it a business domain? A new technology? An old technology? A framework? A mindset?

- After the what and the why comes the how. Do you learn best by watching videos? Reading text? Working through code tutorials? Blogging? A side project? Reading code? Try each of these if you don't know. Find a method which provides useful knowledge that you'll remember.

- Execute. Find the time and the willpower to take the why, the what, and the how, and begin. When you fail, focus on the why to stay motivated. Options for carving out time to learn include scheduling daily time, building something yourself, ordering books on technology for bedtime reading, or participating in online communities.

Figure out how you want to learn, and never stop doing it.

Sincerely,

Dan

Build expert intuition

Kim Schlesinger is a site reliability engineer at Fairwinds. Prior to Fairwinds, she cofounded <div>ersity, a hiring platform focused on diversity, and was an instructor, developer, and curriculum designer for the Web Development Program at Galvanize, a codeschool based in Denver, Colorado. In her spare time, Kim is a CrossFit athlete and the Head of Education and Content for Develop Denver, a two-day conference for developers, designers, strategists, and tech leaders.

Dear new developer,

I know you worked hard to get where you are. You are self-taught, you earned a degree in computer science, or you graduated from a coding bootcamp, and your hard work helped you master the skills required to be a "junior" developer. (I prefer the term early-career developer, but I'll use the terms junior and senior developer.)

Whether you are still searching for your first dev gig, or you've been at your first job for a while, you're probably wondering what it will take for you to be a senior developer. There are lots of factors that contribute to being a "senior," but the most important one is time.

It takes time to become a senior engineer because you are developing what behavioral economist Daniel Kahneman calls "expert intuition." Expert intuition is knowing how the story ends because you've read the book many times before. Expert intuition means that you can see a technical problem and you just know how it can be solved. Expert intuition is the difference between a junior and senior developer.

Kahneman says that the ingredients for this kind of expertise are:

A Regular World + Many Opportunities to Learn + Frequent Feedback = Expert Intuition

Let's take a look at what these things look like for a new developer.

A regular world

A regular world is one where there are a set of rules you can learn. For a new developer, that means a job where you can observe and begin to navigate your company's culture. It also means having an opportunity to write code with a few programming languages, frameworks, and approaches to deploying software. Even if your company's culture isn't great, or you're not writing code in the language you prefer, your early experiences will help you figure out what you do and don't like in a company and if you'd like to specialize in a specific part of the software creation process or remain a generalist.

If you're still searching for a job, you can create a regular world by setting aside time each week to work through exercises on a learning path like Exercism, contributing pull requests to open source projects or civic hacking projects through Code for America, and networking and applying for jobs.

Many opportunities to learn

As a new developer, your most obvious opportunity to learn is to write code and work on technical projects. Definitely do that and know that another way to learn is to observe engineers that are more senior than you.

Pick one colleague you admire, and notice how they learn new concepts or technologies, how they ask questions in meetings, and what they do on a project before they start writing code. Ask to pair with this person, take them out to coffee, and ask them what technologies they're curious about and how they approach writing code. As soon as you identify some of their signature behaviors, start to emulate them.

If you're still looking for a job, find a streamer you like and copy their behaviors. I'm a fan of Coding Garden with CJ and Suz Hinton.

It'll take time for you to make these behaviors your own. However, being intentional with your developer habits and mindsets is a faster path to becoming a senior engineer than other, more conventional, learning opportunities.

Frequent feedback

The final element that will help you develop your expert intuition is getting frequent feedback. You can get feedback from other developers on your code through code reviews and on your technical and nontechnical performance through regular one on ones with your manager. You can reflect and improve on your performance by keeping an end of the day journal where you write down what you learned and how you felt during the day.

It takes time

In June of 2018, I took a job as an apprentice site reliability engineer. Before that, I was a full-time educator and part-time JavaScript developer. I assumed it would take me a few months to figure out how my new company operated and six or so months to get a grasp of cloud computing in AWS and Google Cloud Platform, Docker, Kubernetes, and the wide variety of continuous integration/continuous deployment platforms.

At the time I write this, I'm a year and a half into the job, and although I am more skilled than when I started, there is still so much for me to learn and do. Moving from web development to site reliability engineering is a big transition, and I underestimated how hard it would be. I've made peace with the fact that it will take me years before I will be an expert. New developer, you're starting a new career, and it takes years to grow into your professional self. It takes time, so be patient, and remember the ingredients for developing expert intuition.

Sincerely,

Kim

Teach and learn

Dear new developer,

I'm always thrilled when new developers help others. When they return and mentor at their bootcamp or present at meetups, it helps them and their audience. Everyone has something to teach.

You may think to yourself: "No! I am learning so much right now. I don't know anything. There's no way I could teach anyone something."

False.

There are a number of ways that a developer can teach, even at a job where they are learning something new every day. I've found that learning to do something myself is shallow knowledge, whereas knowing something well enough to explain it to others is a much deeper form of understanding. In the former case, I can gloss over things, as long as it works, but in the latter I really need to understand to explain.

Asking questions is one way to teach. This may seem counterintuitive. How is asking questions teaching? These questions can lead people to reevaluate previous decisions which were made with less than perfect information or perhaps that were made when the system was in a different place. These, if asked from a place of genuine interest, will lead to either you learning about the constraints and choices that led to this decision or the other party learning about other, better options. Here are some questions I've asked:

- Why do you have only one server?
- Why are you using that language for data processing and this one for web development?
- Why are we hosting git on our servers instead of using GitHub?

I always love when a new person joins a team because they are the antidote to the "fish in water" syndrome. Because they're embedded in it all the time, fish don't see water. In the same way, teams don't see inefficiencies. I've lived with solutions for so long that I don't remember why they evolved in the way they did. A new team member asking questions causes me to rethink decisions. One time I led a team that used Trello, a free general-purpose tool, for project management. We'd customized it, built an integration, and added layers of process. A new developer came in and basically said, "why don't we use Jira, a tool built for project management?" Using Jira let us work with instead of against our project management tool.

Another way you can teach is to offer your experience with new technology. You might say something like "what do you think about trying <technology>?" Discuss how using a new tool can help build better software. Chances are high that if you are a new developer, you have experience with newer, popular technologies. Keep an eye out for where they might be a fit but do it tactfully. Don't proclaim "the way we currently do this is bone-headed. We should do it this other way." That's not helpful.

For example, I met someone at a conference who was working to introduce a modern software technique. The software he worked on was written in ColdFusion, an older web technology. The company was profitable. But he thought the software development process could be modernized. He introduced test-driven development (TDD). There was resistance to this new idea among the team. So he was implementing it himself and showing how it produced more robust, maintainable code. His hope was to convince the rest of the team with data and results. He did this after consulting with the team and presumably with the blessing of his manager. You don't want to secretly rewrite a whole subsystem and surprise your team with "improvements" or change the codebase from tabs to spaces (or vice versa) leading to merge conflicts for everyone. Introducing new technologies by dogfooding them yourself can convince skeptics.

Another way to teach is to niche down and find neglected areas of a codebase. Ask other team members "what parts of the code are scary?" Learn them. Work through that code and document what is happening. Bonus points if you write tests. Doing this helps you learn the codebase and become a local expert. Later you can help others understand it.

An aside: Some people are unwilling to learn from people they consider "new" or "junior," but some people have a hard time learning from *anyone*.

All of these require you to both teach and learn, which is as it should be; rarely is anyone solely an educator or a student. Also, as a new developer, be humble because you don't know what you don't know.

When you are starting out, you are unlikely to have the full context for how and why a system or codebase is the way it is. Never trash code, even if team members are doing so. You don't know the constraints under which the code was written. When I am new to a team or system, I couch any suggestions in terms of "This is what I think, based on my knowledge of the system. What do you <person who has been working on the system for a long time> think?"

Humility doesn't mean that you are always the student. Be tactful, ask questions, learn, but realize you have something to teach. Everyone does.

Sincerely,

Dan

What is your woodlot?

Dear new developer,

Gene Logsdon, a farmer who passed away in 2016, was a wise man. In a blog post,[2] he discusses why wood is more valuable than gold:

> *You can't eat gold like you can the bounty of trees in fruits, nuts, maple syrup, and various edible mushrooms and herbal treasures of the woodland. You can't warm yourself with gold. You can't bask in the shade of gold. You can't make fence posts out of gold. A gold house would be mighty expensive. You can't make a windbreak out of gold. You can't make furniture, violins, guitars, wall paneling, picture frames, gun stocks, tomato stakes, flooring, barns, chicken coops, and hog houses out of gold. You can't mulch a garden with gold leaf. Gold does not take in carbon dioxide and give off oxygen to preserve an environment we can live in. Gold does not provide habitat for millions of wild animals and zillions of insects necessary for a sustainable environment. And in fact, you can make methane out of wood much more efficiently than ethanol out of corn. All gold can do is go up and down in price and invariably it turns out to be a poor investment, as many panic buyers learn the hard way.*

In short, it's better to have a skill that can be used multiple ways, like the woodlot, than one which can only be used for one purpose, like gold. Knowing how to learn is a software developer's woodlot. Knowing one particular technology is like owning a bar of gold.

Learning is important because of the constant pace of change. Software is also uniquely reusable. I always tell teams I lead that almost every problem we're facing is a new one, because if it wasn't new, it would have been automated or

---

[2]https://thecontraryfarmer.wordpress.com/2017/12/30/gene-logsdon-wood-is-more-precious-than-gold/

turned into a service or library that we could use or buy. Here are the categories of software development knowledge:

- Domain knowledge
- Theoretical expertise
- Practical knowledge
- Leadership and teamwork skills

Domain knowledge is understanding the real-world problem domain. So, if you've worked, as I have, in a real estate brokerage, you understand how the business works—who pays for what, how money and effort flow, who the main players are, and what they are named. This is useful because you understand how a software system maps to the real world. That makes communication with users and other stakeholders easier and allows you to avoid expensive mistakes made when the application doesn't map to reality.

Domain knowledge changes slowly over the years and decades. I haven't worked in real estate for years, but if I went back, the concepts and major players wouldn't have changed. You can acquire this knowledge by reading and talking to business domain experts. Focusing on a technical problem and solution is a missed opportunity for you to deepen your domain knowledge. If you can, stay in a domain long enough to build understanding. The longer you are steeped in a given area, the more valuable you become, as you gain experience with the concepts and solutions.

Theoretical expertise is the ideas and practices fundamental to software development. I'd put abstractions like algorithms and data structures, specific technologies like distributed systems, database indices, and HTTP, and best practices like automated testing and requirements gathering into this category. This type of knowledge lets you understand a system even if you haven't seen the nuts and bolts of it.

Of course, the type of general technology that is most useful to you depends on your problem area. The technology knowledge needed by a chipset engineer is different than that of a UX designer. This knowledge is good for years. I find the best way to learn this is to read and study classic books and articles, but hands-on debugging is helpful too.

A formal CS degree is useful as well. I don't have one, and every time I must learn new theoretical knowledge, I have extra catching up to do. This catch-up learning requires understanding imposing jargon. Big O notation is an example of this. When I first heard about it, it seemed scary and abstract, but after a bit of study, it's really just counting loops.

Specific technology knowledge is narrowly focused. These are the keywords on job postings and what consultants chase after: Elm or Elixir, Rails or React Native, Kubernetes or KVM. I'm of two minds about this knowledge. On the one hand, if you pick the right one, you will be in demand, which leads to career choices and salary growth. On the other hand, new technologies are constantly released, and keeping up with all of them, let alone gaining expertise, requires large time investments. I also feel like many developers can get up to speed on a new technology in a couple of weeks, at least enough to be effective at making changes to an existing system.

However, I also have sympathy for folks seeking specific expertise. As mentioned, any competent software developer can pick up any language in a short period, but understanding the idiosyncrasies, libraries, and community practices take time. You may find it cheaper to pay someone who has acquired that knowledge elsewhere. As you can imagine, this type of knowledge ages quickly. Videos, conference talks, and tutorials all help me learn specific technologies.

Leadership knowledge is orthogonal to software expertise. Since applications are built by human teams, knowing how to lead engineers toward business goals is a valuable skill. This knowledge includes specific techniques like agile development and "one on ones" and more general topics like how to connect with people and how to navigate politics.

This knowledge has a long half-life and will pay dividends throughout your career. Books and the school of hard knocks have taught me the most about this aspect of software development. One time I was managing a new developer; I'm very goal oriented and I wanted to learn what her goals were. I'm afraid I was a bit too enthusiastic and didn't read her nonverbal signals indicating that wasn't really how she wanted to be managed. This caused team turmoil; I learned that you need to manage employees how they want to be managed, not how you would want to be managed.

Just like the woodlot has many more uses than the pile of gold, learning general skills has more value than knowing any technology or technique.

Sincerely,

Dan

Avoid being an expert beginner

Dear new developer,

An "expert beginner" is an authority with nontransferrable skills. They have been at one organization and have influenced that technology environment so it reflects their knowledge rather than best practices. An expert beginner rarely interacts with the larger software community.

Much like fish isolated in caves become adapted to their environment, a developer who is an expert beginner is intimately familiar with the systems they work with. They can make those systems dance. But just as those fish can't survive in a normal pond, the expert beginner's knowledge also limits them. They'll use tools in ways you shouldn't, be ignorant or dismissive of best practices, and in general build suboptimal software.

The concept of the expert beginner, originally espoused by Erik Dietrich,[3] resonates with me. I've spent most of my career in small companies. That fits best with my desires and my life goals. But I'm acutely aware that as I become more experienced, I am one of the most senior technical people in the room. This would be a problem if I believed that I had all of the answers; this is what the expert beginner believes. You must always be open to new ideas.

An easy way to avoid this fate is to engage with peers in person. Conversations over coffee with former coworkers don't dig as deep technically as they might have when I'd been working with them. But by keeping in touch with my work network, I can avoid the trap of thinking that because I'm at the "local maximum" of software development expertise at a small company, I'm also at the "global maximum."

You can also keep learning by engaging with the local or worldwide software community. Activities I've enjoyed and learned from include:

- Going to a local meetup
- Joining an online tech community
- Reading and writing blogs
- Reading and answering questions on Stack Overflow
- Following smart people on Twitter
- Seeking mentors
- Having lunch with interesting people
- Going to and speaking at conferences

If you have experienced developers on your team, that is a high-bandwidth way to level up: ask to pair with them, pepper them with questions, read pull requests that they file. Be aware that they have their own blind spots, as we all do.

---

[3]https://daedtech.com/how-developers-stop-learning-rise-of-the-expert-beginner/

Unfortunately, not every work environment has senior developers. If that's the case, improve yourself by engaging with the larger software community, and avoid being an expert beginner.

Sincerely,

Dan

Pattern match to be a just-in-time learner

Dear new developer,

In the context of manufacturing, the phrase "just in time" means delivering the right parts to the right plant at the right time. This revolutionized manufacturing. Just-in-time learning means that you learn what you need to know at the right time, that you pick up new knowledge when you need it. This means that you can perform tasks outside your core competency. You may not do them perfectly, since you are learning as you go, but you can get them done. And sometimes you just need to get a task done. An example might be setting up a deployment pipeline for your application. Sure, it'd be great to have an expert around to do this for you, but often there's no one else; either you're on a small team or the expert is unavailable.

Pattern matching helps you learn in a just-in-time fashion. By drawing from your existing store of knowledge, rather than having to start from first principles, you accelerate your ability to deliver. Pattern matching helps you do this by looking at tasks, thinking about how you'd do them in a different context, then mapping the actions to the current situation. As you gain experience, you'll begin to see these patterns.

For example, when I see a new dependency management tool, I know it'll operate similarly to the other dependency management tools I'm familiar with. It will have:

- A dependency tree, usually stored in a text file
- A central online repository, or multiple repositories, where shared code lives
- Private repositories for proprietary code
- Commands to update individual packages or entire application dependencies

Crucially, I also know why this tool exists—to allow software developers to build on top of others' efforts in a repeatable, manageable way. I don't really need to master each dependency manager because I can map between the ones I know (maven and bundler) and the ones I'm less familiar with (composer and npm). I explore by analogy and learn just enough to do what I need to do, which means I'm not overwhelmed by each new tool.

For example, if I need to figure out a way to update a single package using npm, I can search with terms drawn from my knowledge of maven. Pattern matches rely heavily on the power of the Internet and common terminology. When searching, I will use words that span technologies. Sometimes I need to find a translation between two terms that mean similar things, such as function and method. Pattern matching requires knowing how to Google well.

You can apply such matching across software development in general, not just with specific tools. Every language has structures for storing data in memory. Every project has a production environment and a way to deploy code to production. Every system has an architecture.

However, when you pattern match, be aware of your limits. Just because every language has a list data structure doesn't mean that the performance, memory usage, or maintainability characteristics of that list are the same. The analogy helps you get started, but dive in deeper to understand nuances.

Be a just-in-time learner. Focus on what's in front of you and learn how to accomplish that. Look for patterns and analogies between past experience and your current problems.

Sincerely,

Dan

Help, I can't learn something because it is boring!

Dear new developer,

Sometimes you must learn something boring. I know there are times when I've had to schlep, whether when learning a framework that I'll never use again or manually replicating a bug repeatedly in order to fix it. Here are a couple of tips on how to deal with this tedium:

- *Focus on the big picture*—This helps me stay motivated. Why am I doing this? How is it connected to the larger goals of the organization? Who is this going to help when it is finished?

- *Notice the fun parts*—You can't, of course, do only the fun parts, but you can notice them and smile. For example, I am not a front-end developer. I find CSS to be alternatingly frustrating and boring, but there are times when I have to mangle it. Err, I mean modify it. I enjoy learning the basics, like the difference between padding and margin. And it is a good excuse to have a pleasant chat with other team members with expertise in CSS.

- *Take breaks when you need to*—If the deadline isn't tight and there are other tasks on your to-do list, take a break and cross one off. Remember that your career is a marathon, not a sprint.

- *Automate what you can*—Don't go overboard but write a shell script or shell alias. Especially if you're debugging something, this automation will help you focus on the intrinsic work you are doing and can make the whole process less tedious. However, avoid overly elaborate automation—you don't want to take three hours to write a script to automate a task that would have taken you one hour manually and which you won't have to do again.

- *Make sure what you are learning remains relevant*—Depending on how long you've been learning this technology, you may want to make sure what you are doing is still needed. This doesn't apply if you have only been researching for a few hours, but if it has been a few days or weeks, other priorities may take precedence. Be prepared to answer the question "well, how long do you have left?" with some level of confidence.

Sometimes you must learn something that you find boring. Hopefully, these tips will help make it a little easier.

Sincerely,

Dan

Your team will teach you

Dear new developer,

I've always learned more with team members than alone. Other technical people working on the same problems will elevate you, even if they are new developers too. They'll bring different backgrounds from which you can learn, including such know-how as:

- Technical tools like languages and frameworks

- Business domain knowledge

- Approaches to problem-solving

- Understanding of the problem
- Stakeholder empathy

These are all reasons to take a job with a team. The amount you can learn from other people, even those with the same or less experience than you have, is more than you can learn on your own. After all, if each person on the team has one year of experience, and there are three of you, you each collectively have access to three years of experience.

If there are senior people on the team, observe how they work. They aren't perfect, but you can benefit from learning how they operate. If the senior folks are unavailable to meet face to face, you can still read their code and pull requests. Get familiar with `git log` and try to understand their reasoning.

As you work with team members, try to understand and appreciate where they are coming from, especially when they provide different perspectives. For instance, I worked with a small team on an image recognition application, and that was the first time I achieved a real appreciation for the use of a NoSQL database. I'd always dismissed NoSQL solutions before then. Because I worked on a team with different backgrounds than I had, I was able to learn the ins and outs of a new technical stack, which has proven useful since. Your ability to grasp how others solve problems can help the team to arrive at the best possible solution.

Learning from your team members is a great way to access experiences that you can't get or simply haven't had yet.

Sincerely,

Dan

Use an RSS reader

Dear new developer,

Use an RSS reader. By doing so, you'll set up a centralized information hub that you can access when convenient for you. When you run across an interesting source of information like a blog, add it to your reader. Then, whenever a new post is published, you'll be notified. You don't even have to remember the site URL. The RSS reader polls the site and, when there is new content, will display it to you.

RSS stands for Really Simple Syndication and was standardized in the early 2000s. I use the NewsBlur reader, but there are a few good options. It's easy to move between them because the format of the list of monitored sites is standardized.

One of the best things about using an RSS reader is that it lets me go to the content when I want to, rather than having the content come to me, as it would if I were subscribed to a mailing list. It is also a single application to open. Instead of having to go to different places on the Web, I go to one. An RSS reader is similar to Twitter or Reddit, but less noisy, with fewer controversies, more control, and richer content.

RSS readers are not only for keeping track of blogs. You can use a reader to keep tabs on your favorite online community discussions, tags in Stack Overflow, or popular news sites. Using tools, you can convert social media streams such as Twitter searches to RSS feeds and then consume them with your reader.

I primarily read RSS feeds on my phone. Reading on my mobile device takes advantage of scrap moments of time, such as when I'm waiting at an appointment.

Here are some of the types of software development content that I find it useful to subscribe to:

- *Friends or acquaintances who blog*—I know these folks and want to make sure to see whatever they've written. These may be former colleagues or folks I've met at a conference.

- *Corporate announcements*—If I'm using a company's services, I subscribe to their blog. I can then learn about new services, updates, or pricing changes. Among others, I subscribe to the AWS and GCP blogs.

- *Long-form, rarely updated blogs*—There is absolute gold in these articles, which have changed how I think or feel. Charity Majors, for example, has a great blog[4] covering a variety of topics from engineering management to observability. But she posts infrequently. Adding her site to my RSS reader makes sure I won't miss anything.

- *Niche experts*—If I'm interested in learning a specific technology, I subscribe to focused blogs. For example, if I wanted to dive deep into Ruby on Rails, I'd subscribe to Nate Berkopec's blog and the Test Double blog.

- *Companies I want to follow*—Sometimes I'll run across a company and think "wow, that'd be a great place to work." If they have a blog, especially an engineering blog, I subscribe. That way I'll be reminded of them whenever I

---

[4]https://charity.wtf/

visit my reader. The next time I'm looking for a job, I will have a few interesting companies on my radar. RSS is also useful for following your company's competitors.

RSS is a venerable format, but one that can still do great work for you.

Sincerely,

Dan

Listen to podcasts

Dear new developer,

During your day, there are times when your body is occupied, but your mind is not: doing the dishes, exercising, or driving.

With this extra time, listen to podcasts. Most smartphones have an app to download and play them. Good podcasts help you learn by:

- Exposing you to new ideas and concepts
- Giving you an awareness of new technologies and tools
- Letting you learn from others' wisdom and experience

Podcasts are not a replacement for code tutorials or other hands-on practice. Rather, podcasts expose you to new concepts and give you terms for further research. Sometimes just knowing that something exists is enough. For instance, I learned about a Ruby library called graphiti which makes creating APIs trivial from a podcast. I don't need this knowledge right now, but in the future I might. Now I know the gem exists and can read the documentation with simple Google search.

Here are three categories of podcasts to help your development career:

- *Domain specific*—If you work at a startup disrupting the real estate industry, listen to a podcast or two about real estate, such as the BiggerPockets podcast. Car insurance? Fashion? In each case, find focused podcasts. You don't need to be an expert in the business domain, but the more you understand it, the more able you'll be to communicate with subject matter experts about the nuances of the problem space and therefore build the right software.

- *Technology specific*—If you are writing code in Ruby on Rails, listen to podcasts about Ruby and Rails development, such as the Ruby on Rails podcast. The same for

JavaScript, Erlang, or Lisp. These podcasts elevate your development skills in the subject language by exposing you to useful tools, techniques, and libraries, just as I learned about graphiti. I like to email myself new discoveries when I listen to these kinds of podcasts.

- *General software development*—There are a lot of these. Some are more technical, like Software Engineering Radio, and focus on architecture or scalability concerns. Some are less technical and discuss the human side of software development, including leadership and communication styles, such as Authority Issues. These are the podcasts I am least likely to unsubscribe from when I switch jobs, because the topics are broadly applicable to software engineering.

Don't feel that you must listen to every episode—I don't. I pick and choose based on the show notes, topics, and guests. And don't feel bad about unsubscribing when you switch jobs or industries, or even if a podcast is simply no longer of interest.

Podcasts are a great way to get exposed to different software development concepts during downtime.

Sincerely,

Dan

Subscribe to link newsletters

Dear new developer,

Email newsletters can be a great way to learn about a specific domain. Experts gather articles and information about relevant topics and share them with you. They sift through much more of the Internet than you could on your own. These are typically delivered weekly. I've found these for many topics, including software development practices, security, AWS, and career skills.

These newsletters don't take any effort on your part, other than signing up of course. Once a week you receive an email full of links in your inbox. Subscribing is a low-effort way to learn about new technologies, familiarize yourself with an area, and get links to share with your team.

Here are a few tips about email newsletters:

- *Pick and choose*—There are many because developers' attention is valuable. Search around for a bit before you subscribe. Good terms to search for are "<subject area> weekly newsletter" or "<subject area> email newsletter."

- *Read the archives first*—This will give you a preview of the content and the voice of the newsletter.

- *You don't have to read every link*—I find it overwhelming when I receive an email with 50 links. Scroll through it and read only the especially interesting ones.

- *Share the wealth*—Share pertinent links with your online community, your team, or a former colleague.

- *Use it as a source for your RSS reader*—When an information source is linked to that seems worth keeping track of, add it to your RSS reader.

- *Explore*—Use the newsletter to explore a new technology or area of software development. The regular, curated content will introduce you to both jargon, useful for further searching, and people writing well about the topic.

- *Don't be afraid to unsubscribe*—Easy come, easy go. If you don't use a technology any longer, or aren't interested after doing initial research, don't clutter up your inbox. You can always subscribe again if you miss it.

If you are looking for a newsletter for a topic and can't find it, you could also start your own, but mentally prepare to have few subscribers when starting up. TinyLetter is one tool which can help. Plan to spend time finding and curating links.

I find these email lists especially helpful to tune into a tech community. They are a great way to keep on top of what people are talking about without you having to spend any time searching.

Sincerely,

Dan

Read great books about software development

Dear new developer,

You won't learn the latest development techniques from books. Those are described online in blogs or videos—or possibly in papers, if you work in an area where academia is doing research.

Nor will you learn specific approaches that you can put to immediate use to solve a current work problem from books. That kind of assistance is found in docs, GitHub issues, or Stack Overflow.

What you will learn from the great books of software engineering are timeless practices. You'll learn how to dig deeply into a topic and how to take what is in a book and apply it.

I've joined discussion groups about software books, which can be a fun way for people to share their experiences. Such groups also hold me accountable; sometimes great books, like *Gödel, Escher, Bach*, can be hard to finish.

Here are three software books to get you started:

- *The Mythical Man-Month*—This book covers what is arguably one of the first major modern software projects. This book explores the difficulties of building software. It's the source of the commonly cited fact that when a project is late, adding more developers will increase communication needs and thus delay it further. It is sobering reading when you compare what was done decades ago to today's practices.

- *The Pragmatic Programmer*—This book discusses software best practices and ways to level up your personal software development skills. It has a great set of checklists.

- *Refactoring*—This volume explores refactoring, a specific type of software maintenance. In the same way that you need to take care of your car, you need to maintain software. How to do it, when to do it, how to talk about it—these are all covered.

I read these books in dead-tree format. I find it best to have a pen so I can underline statements that make a lot of sense to me or that I want to consider further. I dog-ear relevant sections. And, unlike a great novel, I don't speed through them. One chapter a day is moving fast.

Finally, finding good books to read is a great way to connect with your team or community. Ask engineers who you respect what books they'd recommend reading. Reading such books deepens your understanding of the craft of software.

Sincerely,

Dan

Listen actively

Dear new developer,

Listening with focus and intention is a great way to learn. When you can really dive deep on what a fellow team member knows, whether in a chance encounter or in a meeting, you'll learn so much. Here's how I listen with focus and intention.

First, stop multitasking. Close the chat system and your email. If you're in person, shut your computer. As best as you can, set aside all your worries, concerns, and to-dos. You'll be able to pick them up again after the conversation, I promise.

Then, take notes. I use my computer if this is a video chat. If I'm in person, I use pen and paper. What should you take notes on? This isn't a college lecture, so you don't need to capture everything. Write down salient points, ah-ha moments, and terms that you might want to review in the future. Note the date of the conversation as well.

As someone is talking, I write down concepts or terms I don't understand. You want to capture these in the moment, but don't interrupt the speaker. When I am listening, I take each statement and make sure I understand it. If not, I capture a note. It doesn't have to be a long one, just enough to remind me of my question.

When the speaker reaches a natural stopping point, or if they ask for questions, I reach for my notes. I try to provide context. I'll say something like "you were talking about the OAuth process and you mentioned pixie something. What is that?"

If it is a smaller group, I may interrupt more often. I'll often rework what they said in my own words so I can be sure I understand it. "Can I repeat what you just said to make sure I understood it? You're saying that for the basic plan, everything, even the database, lives on one server. Is that correct?"

With active listening, you interact with the speaker. However, you want to tweak this interaction based on the context. If it is you and a teammate, then the conversation can be participatory. You can break in whenever there's a pause for clarification. If it is a company-wide meeting, there'll be less interaction. You may still want to take notes, but the follow-up may be additional research or conversations with team members rather than questioning the speaker.

If the conversation is happening over a video chat or conference call, then you have more options. I like to record these if possible. Then, if needed, I can go back and figure out what was said. Make sure you get permission to record. And if you are on a video chat, turn on your video. Even though video isn't as high bandwidth as in-person conversation, you can still pick up contextual clues from it. Is the speaker rolling their eyes as they cover a particular topic? Are they frowning? Smiling? All these are useful nonverbal signals that should inform your responses. They're all absent if you don't have video turned on.

If a conversation results in a decision or assigns folks tasks, I write up a summary and send it over email. This allows everyone to be clear on any required actions. If, on the other hand, it is an informational discussion and other team members may be interested in the topic, writing up a document and putting it online is a good idea. But both of these outputs should be secondary to listening and understanding what is said.

Sincerely,

Dan

Learn two languages

Dear new developer,

When you know one programming language, you can get a lot done, especially if the language is prevalent. For example, in web development, the dominant language is JavaScript. In system programming, it's C. These languages will be around forever, and you'll always be able to get a job if you know them.

You can also have a great career with niche language knowledge. You might have to search a bit harder to find a job, though. Examples of such languages include ClojureScript for web development or Nim for systems programming.

Knowing only one language is like living in the same town all your life. You can be happy and productive. Yet exposure to a different city expands your mind, illustrates divergent living patterns, and helps you understand the strengths and weaknesses of your hometown. Sometimes what we assume are universal truths are simply what we are familiar with.

Software engineers are similar. They are often dogmatic about the virtues of technologies and frameworks, simply because they know them. We also are relatively quick to judge, sometimes with no more justification than the latest blog post we've read. This snap judgment also occurs because we must regularly make decisions about technologies with imperfect information. But you should not put down things you don't understand.

I cut my teeth writing Perl. I wrote a lot of it for my first job. Then I wrote Java. The first Java classes I wrote were, to be charitable, not idiomatic. For instance, rather than using classes, I leveraged hash maps and lists for all my data structures. I remember another engineer reviewing my code and commenting "that looks a lot like Perl written in Java." I didn't know any better, so I'd mapped the solution from my first language onto the second.

Learning a second programming language will:

- Let you see the strengths and weaknesses of your first language. Every language has these, but when you have no basis for comparison, they're harder to see.

- Inform the code you write in language #1 with concepts from the new language. For instance, Perl supported classes, and using classes in Java made it easier to see their usefulness.

- Make it easier to learn a third language, should you choose. You'll see what is common between languages and what is unique.

- Illustrate different approaches to common problems. How does each language deal with encapsulation? With dependency management?

- Teach you how languages fit certain problems better than others. Perl is fantastic for text processing. Java is better for large-scale systems.

- Make you less passionate about your first language. This may seem like a strange benefit, but learning multiple languages reinforces the fact that a programming language is only a tool. You shouldn't fall in love with a tool.

- Make it clear what you understand about language #1. If you can't implement a solution in language #2 that you wrote in language #1, did you really understand it?

When you are learning the second language, it can be helpful at the start to have a mental map between language #1 and language #2. "I know that there's a way to iterate over a list in Perl, so there must be a way to do so in Java." This will also help you learn common software terms, such as "iterate." Knowing these helps with searching the Web.

Which new language should you learn? That depends on where you want to take your career. Ask your team to see if there is more than one language used in your employer's systems. If you want to work with data, learning SQL, a database query language, is a good idea. If you want to work at a certain company, find out what languages they use and learn one.

You can also learn a new language just for fun. For me, a side project is a great way to dig into a new language and take it beyond the tutorials. Tutorials teach me setup and syntax, but to really learn a language, I need to use it for a task where I'm not simply following instructions. By reading the docs and searching the Web, I map past experiences and the written word to my current problem space. I then really start to understand how to use a language. Some examples of mind-bending languages that might be fun to learn are Haskell, OCaml, Prolog, BASIC, and C.

The benefits of "learning a second one" apply not just to languages but all other parts of the software development process. Learn at least two of everything—databases, frameworks, development methodologies. The increase in perspective is worth the extra effort.

Sincerely,

Dan

In conclusion

As a developer, you'll need to learn throughout your career. Over the years as technology has changed, I have spent time, energy, and money making sure I understood the shifting landscape. At the start of your career, there's a lot to learn, but you start building good habits.

At the same time, it's worth acknowledging that you can't learn everything. The world of software is too vast. When you reach the limits of your knowledge, reach out to team members and your communities for help.

Mistakes

Ah, mistakes. I've made so many of them. Mistakes are one part of growing as a developer. If you can do your job perfectly, you aren't pushing your limits. That's the way you grow.

Now, I'm not advocating making mistakes on purpose. I'm just suggesting you take on challenges that you fear you won't be able to accomplish. I've done this many times in my career, from the first time I ran a meeting to taking on a developer relations role. In the latter case, I had to learn how to bridge between marketing and engineering, as well as become comfortable communicating with developers outside my organization. In any unfamiliar situation, you will make mistakes. How you handle them is more important than the fact you make them.

In this chapter, I go over some of the mistakes I've made, including dropping a table in a production database, and cover how to handle failure.

Get used to failure

Dear new developer,

I was chatting with someone who was about to graduate from a bootcamp. I asked him what his advice to a new developer would be. He said that it would be "get used to failure and get used to working through it." How true!

I often tell colleagues working on a problem that if it were easy, someone would have already solved it. When you are trying to fix something in an application, the problem hasn't been solved within your organization—at least not in a way that you are aware of. Therefore, you'll be exploring a new

D. Moore, *Letters to a New Developer*, https://doi.org/10.1007/978-1-4842-6074-6_8

approach. Failure is part of such exploration. Just as scientists limit their scope of inquiry so they can conduct useful experiments, you'll narrow down the problem so that you can most easily find or build a solution. But the most rigorously planned experiments fail. So will you.

New developer, software engineers face additional complexities that scientists do not. The tools that software developers use are themselves software and are being developed to boot. Imagine trying to build a house when the hammers and saws are morphing while in use. A software solution which worked in the past may be suboptimal now.

The real world that scientists try to understand doesn't constantly change. The business world that software developers work within transforms due to internal authority or external dependency. This is an intrinsic difficulty of software development.

As a developer, you face onerous problems in a tough environment. You need to get used to failure, both at the micro and macro levels. You must persevere. You need to be tenacious and realize that through continued effort you'll eventually solve your problem.

Recognize the frustration that failure can lead to. Realize that everyone is going through it. A coach taught me that running is hard for everyone, whether you are running a five-minute mile or a ten-minute mile. The same is true for software development. Learning something new is difficult and frustrating, whether it's your first application or the intricacies of a new build and deployment process for your twentieth. Get used to failure and remember that everyone else encounters it too.

What about problems you tackle which have been solved, but with solutions of which you are unaware? Back in the dark ages before Internet access was widespread, dissemination of software knowledge was slow. It happened via email, bulletin boards, journals, and books. Now we have Google and other search engines as well as Stack Overflow. These help you learn popular software systems such as the NGINX web server or MySQL database server. I've yet to see a great solution for sharing internal knowledge, such as how your custom business application works. You should document these systems as best you can to help others with problems you have already solved.

Once you have a problem even partially defined, resist the temptation to dive in and work on a solution. Rather, pop your head up and ask around to see if anyone has solved your problem—or even one-third of it. You may or may not reuse their solution, but it will inform your code either way.

Sincerely,

Dan

Making mistakes is okay

Dear new developer,

One time, not too many years ago, I was using git. I had used it for personal projects before, but this was my first time in a team setting. We were using a common git branching model. This meant I was creating feature branches and committing code to them.

Often I would be working on the same feature branch as a colleague. The first couple of times I did so, I checked out this shared branch using git checkout -b branchname. I'd then pull down the remote branch: git pull origin branchname and get to work.

Do not do this.

Using these commands will check out a branch named branchname, but the new branch will be based on whatever branch was previously checked out. The pull will then merge the remote branch into your current workspace. You'll get the code you want to work on, but there will be other changes lurking. This is no good!

The correct way to pull down a remote feature branch is to run git fetch origin branchname and then git checkout branchname.

I point this out not because I'm trying to teach you version control, though it is a great tool to learn. Rather, this was a big mistake on my part. I don't think any code escaped into production, but my error confused other team members and could have been very bad. It's one of the many mistakes I've made in my career. These happen to everyone. It's important to learn how to handle them.

First, find out exactly what the oversight was. You need to understand it so you can avoid repeating it. This may involve a conversation with another team member, research, or both.

Second, acknowledge that you made the error. If you work in an environment where you cannot acknowledge missteps, make plans to leave as soon as possible. When you are acknowledging the mistake, don't wail and beat yourself up. Saying "oh, wow, I really screwed up that git branch stuff. Sorry!" lets team members know you made a mistake and that you are adult enough to recognize it.

Third, clean it up. You may need some help, but part of taking responsibility for your errors is fixing them as best as you can.

Fourth, avoid making the same misstep again. This may involve keeping a notebook, writing a blog post, or committing the correct behavior to memory. What you need to do depends on how you learn and the size of the mistake. Everyone makes mistakes, but you want to avoid making the same one repeatedly. Bonus points if you document or script the correct action so that other folks can benefit from your new knowledge.

Mistakes happen. It's okay. Don't pretend you don't make errors; instead own up to them, learn from them, and make different ones next time.

Sincerely,

Dan

Mistakes are forgiven, hiding them is not

Dear new developer,

We all make mistakes. Yes, this is not news, but I think it is worth repeating.

We all make mistakes.

I have made them, you have made them, senior developers have made them, your boss has made them, interviewers have made them. Even CEOs make them regularly.

If you only remember one thing about mistakes, let it be this: never ever hide them. Now, that doesn't mean you should publish every error on your blog or your LinkedIn profile. We should tell the truth, but that doesn't mean saying every sentence which crosses your mind. In the same way, you should divulge your oversights carefully.

The people who need to know about your error should be told. Exactly who needs to know depends on the size and scope of your mistake. If in doubt about who needs to know, ask your mentor, your supervisor, or a trusted teammate. Don't lollygag when examining your oversights. When you discover a mistake, take the following steps.

First, confirm it is really a mistake. Don't be the child who cried wolf. Avoid making an error about a mistake. Take a look at what you think you did wrong from several perspectives. If this wasn't a misstep, then you're fine. If it was, the next step is ameliorate it.

Think of a plan for fixing the mistake. You may need help from other team members, depending on the severity of the mistake. It may mean shutting down part of a system to mitigate the impact. You may need both an immediate plan to fix the consequences of the error and a long-term plan to prevent it from happening again. I once worked on a system where an inadvertent change in the content management system exposed a server which wasn't ready for a large amount of traffic. High load brought this server to its knees, crashing the site. The immediate fix was removing the code change. The long-term fix was making sure that if any code changes of that type occurred in the future, an automated system would notify a developer who could investigate and, if needed, roll back those changes.

Think about who is affected and the scope of the error. Then communicate the issue and the plan to fix it to those parties. This communication often requires planning as well.

Exposing your mistakes in this way is uncomfortable. When I was at a startup, I wrote billing software for clients. There were times when I made an error. I remember one time I had to email or call each customer whose billing I had screwed up. It was unpleasant. But they understood and appreciated the transparency and honesty.

What is the alternative to being upfront about mistakes? Hiding your missteps and pretending they never happened? Well, not really. Doing so ensures you won't learn from your mistakes. It also means that your users or boss may discover the oversight and bring it to your attention in a less pleasant manner.

Making mistakes is fine. Hiding them is not.

Sincerely,

Dan

Don't make the same mistake twice

Dear new developer,

We all screw up. After all:

> *To err is human...*
>
> —Alexander Pope

A few years ago, I was working with a new version control system. I didn't take the time to understand exactly how to use it, but instead mapped a few concepts in my head and started writing code. A few days in, my branch was missing code present in a coworker's branch.

Turns out I'd been pulling down remote branches incorrectly and creating new branches instead. Whoops!

I made that mistake once and only once. I took two different steps to correct the issue. First, I learned the right command. Second, I realized that a version control system is important enough to invest time to learn. I therefore spent some time reading and playing around with this new piece of software, including learning some common commands.

Here are ways you can avoid repeating errors:

- When you make a mistake, make sure you understand what the mistake was.

- Find out if the oversight was simple, or, as in the case I mentioned earlier, there was a second- or third-order issue to investigate and resolve.

- Write down your misstep so that you and others can avoid it in the future. You could use a notebook or a blog, whatever works.

Errors occur; no one is perfect. But the goal is to always make new mistakes, not the same mistake again and again.

Sincerely,

Dan

Don't be afraid to "fail"

Cierra Nease graduated from the General Assembly bootcamp and is currently employed by AWS.

Dear new developer,

"Failures" as a new developer are plenty—but you might be asking, why is "failures" in quotes? To fail something is dependent upon one's perspective. The only true failure is to quit working toward success. Every failure brings a small success in that you learn what the right answer is not. How can you problem-solve without a way of marking off solutions that do not work? A failure is simply a solution that didn't work at that specific time.

We can all talk about how learning and growth come from having failures, but it's hard to remember that when you feel like you are a failure. Failures do not inherently make the person a failure, and it can be hard to make that distinction in the moment. Sometimes we need someone else to remind us of this.

I've had a lot of people in life reiterate this concept to me. The most recent person was a fellow developer named Mike on the Denver light rail. It's funny what will happen when people participate in communicating and interacting with each other, but that is for another letter entirely. For now, let's go back to Mike. Mike overheard me talking to another passenger about being in a bootcamp. When I finished my conversation, he handed me a card and said he'd love to answer any questions I have about becoming a developer. I elaborated on some of my bootcamp experience, which happens to be full of failures.

Mike expressed his number one piece of advice for any developer, telling me "whatever you do, don't be afraid to fail." We started talking about this in depth, and it really resonated with me for the rest of the evening. As a new developer, you really only see senior developers' successes. Each developer goes through their own learning process which does include failures.

The failures that lead to success don't stop when you become a "better" developer. If you are looking for a point when you quit failing as a developer, then you are looking for the wrong thing. The more you fail, the more you learn. The more you learn, the more you grow. The more you grow, the better the developer you become.

As a newer developer, I look forward to all of the opportunities to learn, grow, and accept my failures as the wrong solution instead of accepting them as a personal characteristic.

Sincerely,

Cierra

That time I dropped a production table

Dear new developer,

When you use SQL (Structured Query Language) to interact with your database, how do you write delete statements?

A delete statement looks something like this: `delete from table_name where column_name = 'foo';`. I usually write it in this order:

1. `delete`
2. `delete where column_name = 'foo';`
3. `delete from table_name where column_name = 'foo';`

This is a bit tedious because after step 2 I have to arrow back to add the `from` clause. But it prevents me from making a mistake and sending a command such as `delete from table_name;` by accident. That command, without a where clause, deletes all the data in your table. This is not usually what you want.

One time I did just that. I accidentally deleted all the data from one table in a production database. The table held all the information needed to charge customers. Luckily, my database was being backed up every 5 minutes. I was able to recover the data before any charges failed.

I took the following steps to recover from dropping this production, revenue-generating table:

- I took a deep breath.

- I diagnosed what parts of the application would be affected and when.

- I wrote a message on the team chat channel documenting what had happened and the possible customer impact.

- After examination, I knew what I deleted was used only once a day. Therefore, I didn't have to put the application in maintenance mode to prevent further damage.

- I reviewed the documentation on restoring the database from the backup.

- I carefully restored the missing data.

- I communicated that systems were back to normal to the team.

- I updated the documentation based on what I'd learned.

- I wrote a blog post about removing data from production tables.

Anyone can make a mistake. I was the expert on this system as I had written the entire application. No one knew it better than I. At the time, I had about 15 years of professional software experience.

The first step in handling a mistake is taking whatever actions you need to take to remain calm. Taking that deep breath, remembering that I'd set up backups, and knowing I could fix the problem were the first steps to actually remediating the issue. You need to keep your head clear and make sure your mistake doesn't get compounded; that will only make the situation worse.

Sincerely,

Dan

You're going to put some plates in toasters

Dear new developer,

I love this insightful tweet from Nora Jones, an engineer who has worked at Netflix and Slack:[1]

---

[1]https://twitter.com/nora_js/status/1224905963804606467

My friend taught her son how to use the toaster recently. she explained all the notches to him, how each turn on the knob increases the minute count, etc. She received a text from her husband the next day saying that he found a plate in the toaster.

You don't know what you don't know.

When I think back over the years, I am amazed at how many tasks I can now do easily, but which baffled me at the beginning of my career. These include both technical and nontechnical undertakings. This list includes, but is not limited to:

- Navigating files and directories
- Examining an HTTP call at multiple levels of abstraction
- Estimating and then determining the performance of an application
- Refactoring a system
- Architecting an application
- Running a meeting
- Planning a project
- Exiting vi

The road is long. And there's a lot to learn.

By the way, I still put plates in toasters periodically. Recently at work, I energetically revised a planning document, adding what I thought was a ton of insight and value. I was told later the value I added was actually negative and that I'd done more harm than good to the organization's goals. Man, was that a humbling and learning experience. Honestly, that was more like putting a fork in an electrical socket than putting a plate in a toaster.

Much of what I know, I know at a high level of abstraction. Then, when I need to know details, I dive in using resources like Google, Stack Overflow, or a mentor. Just knowing that a solution or library exists means that I can leverage all the learning resources available if I see a situation where it may apply. I also do a lot of pattern matching, where I compare how one system or process worked and apply that knowledge, thoughtfully, to a new problem.

When you find yourself floundering, take a deep breath, forgive yourself, and dig in to learn. You can acquire foundational competence with time and study. But until then, and even after, you'll be putting plates in toasters.

Sincerely,

Dan

What do I do when I see someone making a mistake?

Dear new developer,

Somewhere, sometime, someone will do something wrong. It happens more often than you think. That person might even be you or me.

When someone makes a mistake, I want to correct them, to show them the benefit of my hard-won experience and enlighten them. Usually, this impulse is incorrect and counterproductive.

What should I do instead of jumping in and letting them know they are headed toward Errorville?

- *Consider whether I have all the context*—This is actually an easy question to answer: I don't. I strive to remember that from their perspective, their choices make sense.

- *Make sure I really understand the issue they are facing*—Sometimes, I appreciate their choice once I have more information. Other times, my questions cause them to make different decisions or revise their thinking.

- *Think about the ramifications of a poor decision*—It's better to let someone choose the wrong course of action when the stakes are low. We've all made mistakes and that's a great way to learn. However, the higher the stakes, the more likely I should intervene, at least to discuss the options.

- *Contemplate my role*—Is this person a peer? An old friend? An ex-colleague? A mentor? A mentee? Someone I've just met? Different relationships and trust levels lead to different tolerances for my opinion.

In short, rather than explaining to someone why they are wrong, I need to stop and think about the entire situation, including what I've missed, what the consequences of the oversight might be, and how welcome my advice is.

Sincerely,

Dan

The despair of ineptitude

Dear new developer,

I recently learned a new skill. And, like many people are when they are starting out, I wasn't good at it. The skill, if you must know, was writing with a certain tone for a corporate blog. But the lessons apply irrespective of the actual task.

I don't like being inept—especially since the task was adjacent to blogging, an activity I was quite experienced at. I would get feedback on how to improve this aspect or that aspect of my writing. I understood the feedback, it made sense, but I felt like a failure. I felt shame. It honestly pissed me off. But after the shame passed, I recognized the comments were correct; I wasn't producing what was needed.

It's important to acknowledge that it's okay to fail and that it's okay to be bummed about it. We're all human and emotions are part of the package. When the shame passed, I had a couple of choices. I could keep trying to improve. Or I could decide that, hey, maybe this wasn't the right task for me to do.

How do you decide when you are faced with these two options? You should examine how important this task is to the organization and who else, if anyone, can do it or help you do it. Here are some questions to think about:

- How core is this task to your job?
- How important is solving this problem to the company?
- How long do you think it'll take you to get good at this?
- Do you enjoy it? Do you want to be good at it?
- Is there another way to solve the problem for the company?
- Is there someone at your company who can help teach you?

Now, this introspection is good for you to do. But it isn't just your opinion on these questions that matters. Discuss these issues with your manager, possibly in a one on one. If you have a skills gap that is keeping you from doing a key part of your job, you want to resolve this quickly. If the support from your manager is missing, then you are in a tough situation; I'd try to understand why, but that's a hard conversation to have. Either way, you should confront your ineptitude directly. The conversation will determine how and where to invest your time.

This discussion may also lead to a deeper understanding of the task, a shift in roles or duties, or, in some circumstances, a departure from the company. The former options are more likely than the last, but layoffs and firings happen.

The despair when you are bad at something is understandable. Just don't beat your head against the wall trying to get better. Step back and be strategic about your efforts.

Sincerely,

Dan

Admit your weaknesses

Dear new developer,

I once had a conversation with my manager. It went a bit like this: "Hey, sometimes I can be overly direct and it comes off as me being a jerk. I've been told I've been condescending by coworkers. I'm working on being more empathetic and less blunt but if you see behavior like this from me, please let me know."

At one time in my career, I wouldn't have had the confidence to admit this. I had this discussion because I'm aware of my weaknesses, and I want to own them. Sharing them with your manager can only help if you have a good manager. If you don't have a good one, then you have bigger problems. (I'd start interviewing.) A good supervisor can help you grow and place you in situations where your strengths will shine and your weaknesses won't be fatal.

In what kind of skills might you have challenges? There are two dimensions to think about.

First, consider whether the weakness is innate, such as my bluntness. Or is it a skill you can learn, like Python?

You can learn a lot, often more than you think. It's a matter of energy, desire, and time. That said, you may choose to accept a weakness because you don't want to make that investment. I don't care much about precisely following a design down to each pixel placement. This lack puts some developer jobs off limits. I worked in positions where that skill mattered before I determined I didn't care, though. Don't write off a skill too quickly.

If a competence is required for a position and you have an innate lack of that skill, consider another job. Barring that option, be proactive in addressing the weakness. This includes, as I did, informing your manager of the issue and then working to ameliorate the problem.

Another dimension to consider is how important the skill is to your job. Is it very important? Do you have stage fright but must speak in public? Or only tangentially related—you are an engineer who doesn't enjoy writing and need to occasionally publish blog posts?

The more core this competence is to your job, the more proactive you should be in overcoming the obstacle—find a way to improve the skill or shift jobs.

When should you have this conversation about such challenges or skills gaps? Not in the job interview, that's for sure. In the job interview, you should be putting your best foot forward, not talking about your weaknesses. If they ask you about a weakness, they really want to hear about how you overcame one.

However, in private, you should consider how your deficiencies affect your ability to succeed in this potential position. If there's a mismatch, especially if you lack the desire to overcome it, you might want to reconsider this job.

Also, do not dwell on challenges in your performance review. That process should display progress toward career goals, justifying promotions or new opportunities. However, if there's been discussion of deficiencies and you've made changes to address them, discuss that professional growth.

I think the best time to have the conversation about your weaknesses with your manager is when:

- You have a clear idea about your weaknesses.

- You know how they will affect your ability to do your job.

- You have a plan to ameliorate their effects.

- You have been on the job at least a month or two and have achieved a couple of wins.

- You trust your manager.

If the preceding list is true, you will be in a good position to frankly discuss the challenges and take steps to improve. It's best to do this in a face-to-face conversation.

I have had conversations with others who were less willing to have such discussions because in the past this had negatively affected their professional careers. In particular, people who were not white men discovered that revealing weaknesses was counterproductive. If this is a worry, discuss the situation with a trusted former colleague or mentor.

If you can't have this dialogue with your manager, at the least, think about it yourself. On paper, examine your deficiencies and how they interact with your current position. You may find that it is suited to you, in which case, congratulations.

You may, with reflection, find an area to work on. For example, I've thought "man, I really need to get better at listening before I talk." Congratulations again. You have your marching orders on how to improve yourself.

Finally, you may find that your current job is perversely aligned with your weaknesses, in which case, take a look around.

Sincerely,

Dan

In conclusion

Mistakes are natural and part of the learning process. When a profession is as young and fast moving as software development, there's a lot of room for error.

Of course, missteps should be avoided where possible. But when you make a mistake, take responsibility, fix the oversight, share the knowledge, and take steps to make sure neither you nor anyone else makes that mistake again.

Your Career

Most people don't write code just for fun, though programming can be a joy. They do it because it's a good job. One position leads to another, and soon you have a career in software development.

It happened to me.

Your progression as a software engineer is in your hands. There is no licensing authority. The equipment required to learn a new skill is often an Internet connection, a computer, and time. The scope of software engineering work is wide. Embedded systems running elevators, web applications helping people with their jobs, or gigantic globe spanning architectures—all these are built by software developers. If you consider the rapid evolution of the state of the art in software development as well, the possibilities are endless and shifting. You need to determine your career goals and work toward them.

In this chapter, we'll cover such topics. There'll be tactical letters about interviews and one on ones. We'll also look at strategic choices such as ignoring the sound and fury of the Internet and the value of authenticity.

Favor learning over earning

Dear new developer,

I suggest that the first job you take be the one with the highest learning potential, not the largest salary. Positions which aren't as lucrative will set you up for success later in your career.

© Dan Moore 2020

D. Moore, *Letters to a New Developer*, https://doi.org/10.1007/978-1-4842-6074-6_9

Of course, this means the best job for you depends on what you want to learn. If you want to experience working directly with clients, a consulting company is a great place to start. If you want to experience autonomy, rapid change, and chaos, join a startup. If you want to work on deep technical problems, consider a large company with more complex systems.

If you are the sole technical team member, you might be paid more but will learn less. If the plan is to add team members, this may be an adequate situation, if temporary. However, if the business doesn't grow as expected, the team may not grow either.

If you work alone, beware of stunting your growth. It's hard to improve when you don't have other team members to challenge your ideas. Meetups and online communities can help with this, but nothing beats a teammate working in the same codebase.

No one dislikes money. I like money, and I bet you do too. But over-optimizing for initial salary rather than exploring your options is a foolish choice. You may have constraints—family obligations, student loans—but within those, look for teams that will help you improve. Ask about growth during interviews—and not just formal plans; look for results. Did your interviewer start with the company as a new developer and grow into their current role? Are there team members a few years ahead of you in their careers at this organization?

The goal of your first few jobs should be to learn as much as you can. By doing so, you invest in yourself. You'll make more intelligent choices later, be more valuable to future employers, and have a better idea of what you like. When you have a choice, pick the job where you will learn the most.

You don't have to know right away what kind of education you seek, either. In fact, your first few jobs might be very dissimilar. In the first decade of my career, I worked at a consulting company, then as a contractor, then at a startup, then again as a contractor (startups, as mentioned, are chaotic), then at a small product company.

In each case, I learned more about what I liked in a company, a boss, and a business domain.

Sincerely,

Dan

You will never be in a better position to leave a bad job than before you start

Dear new developer,

Interviewing is a two-way street. That means that you, the candidate, need to be evaluating your employer as much as they are assessing you. Yes, you need a job, but your employer needs your skills; that's why they are hiring.

You'll never have more leverage with a company than you do as a candidate. Why? Because when you are interviewing, you can talk to multiple potential employers. If someone acts like a jerk during an interview, it's a hassle, yes. But compare that to having the same person as your manager. In the latter case, you'll be looking for a new job during your precious weekends, at night when you're exhausted, or during your lunch hour. Or worse, you'll stay in a job where you are miserable.

If they don't treat you well during the interview process, when they're trying to convince you to join the team, how will they conduct themselves when you are an employee and don't have any options other than finding a new job?

This means you must invest time to learn about possible future employers. Search the Web for information—just realize that you may need to take what you find with a grain of salt. I once published a blog post about the development process at my employer—how information was transmitted from client to project manager to developer, how the work was done, and how project status made its way back to the client. The post wasn't a lie, exactly, but it documented how the process worked when everything went swimmingly. And, unfortunately, things didn't always go well. Plus, last I checked, it was posted on the company website, even though I know the process has evolved.

Job descriptions also can be misleading. In fact, I'd say in the job descriptions I've written, about 30% of the description didn't apply to the candidate I hired. What? The extra text was there because I was seeking perfection, but I have never hired anyone with all of the desired skills. Every potential employee is missing a chunk of what's needed; it's just a question of which 30% they don't have. I always leave the extra requirements in to attract candidates with different strengths and weaknesses. It's frustrating, but hiring is frustrating for everyone involved. In any case, once you become an employee, the job will also change based on your skills, interests, and company needs.

To learn about how things work at a possible employer, reach out to people you've met in your network and ask. Look on LinkedIn to see if you have any connections, however tenuous, who have worked at this company. Ask these folks about the good and the bad of this organization. You are going to spend a lot of waking hours at your job, so spend the time before you interview.

Interviews are hard to do well. They are designed to extract as much information as possible in a short time period. Companies want an accurate hire/no hire decision. Good employers, however, want a bidirectional information exchange. This can happen in a few ways: by allowing plenty of time for questions during the interview, having a discussion in a casual environment like lunch, or having individual contributors on the team participate in the interview.

During the interview, if the schedule doesn't allow time for your questions, make sure your interviewer knows you have some. If it hasn't already been mentioned, about 15 minutes before the interview is scheduled to end, say something like "I want to be respectful of your time. The interview is scheduled to end in 15 minutes or so. Is this a good time to ask you some questions?" If they don't respond politely to this request, well, that's more good data.

Make sure you have a couple of good questions. My favorites vary based on who is interviewing me, but I'll often ask these:

- What are the best parts of your job and this company?
- What are current challenges you or the company face?
- Why do you believe in this company?
- What does success look like for this position?

These are all good standbys. However, don't ask them if they've already been answered earlier in the interview process. You can incorporate a previous answer into a question, though. This illustrates your attention to detail: "You mentioned earlier that the upgrade to Kubernetes 1.16 was a large challenge for the team. I was wondering if it was because of communication difficulties or a particular technical issue?"

A company's nonverbal signals provide a wealth of data about how your potential employer operates:

- Is the interviewer prepared and respectful?
- Does the interview start on time?
- Is it a real conversation or are you being grilled?
- Does the interviewer appear happy and enthusiastic?
- Is the company communicative regarding deadlines and expectations or are there surprises?
- Does the company ghost you?
- Do people do what they say they are going to do during the interview process?

- Are they flexible during the interview—what happens when something unexpected arises?

- How do they respond to your questions?

- Do they keep in touch after the interview until you're either hired or passed on?

- Do they ask you to do a large take-home project, especially without compensation?

These all paint a picture about the company and the position. Note that none of these signals relate directly to the technology or work you'll be doing. That is important as well, but the context in which you work is crucial. If you are being paid $200,000 per year in a job that makes you miserable, you will be unhappy. In contrast, if you are paid a yearly salary of $100,000 working with a team and a project that you enjoy, you will be happy. These numbers assume that you can live well on either salary—feel free to double the numbers if that isn't the case.

You will never have more power in the employer/employee relationship than when you are interviewing. Even though it is stressful to have no income, this is the point you have the most optionality to pursue a different job. One exception worth noting is when the job market is bad and you're looking for your first position. In that case, I'd recommend taking any position working with software. It's far easier to find another engineering job when you've had any amount of professional experience.

Poor interview treatment indicates, in my experience, a general lack of regard for employees. This leads to other unpleasantness, such as no commitment to or budget for professional development and considering developers "resources" to be shunted between projects.

You will never be in a better position to leave a job that isn't a fit than before you start. An interview is the right time to make sure you learn enough to avoid jobs that aren't for you.

Sincerely,

Dan

Pick a flaw, any flaw

Dear new developer,

Every company has its warts, also called flaws, issues, problems, or challenges. I have never met anyone who worked for the perfect company. Join an organization with your eyes wide open and choose the warts you can live with. You may be able to help solve some issues, but others are permanent.

Some are fundamental parts of the company's business model. For example, I have worked for multiple consulting companies. I hated keeping track of hours, but this task was core to the company's economic model; developer hours were the product the consulting companies sold and therefore had to be precisely tracked.

One wart to avoid is an indifferent team—one punching the clock and only trying to get through the week. If a company is full of people who don't care, you'll have trouble fixing anything else. Customers will be an afterthought. Work will drag. It's unfortunate, but places like this exist.

That's not to say that a place where people care will be only unicorns and cotton candy; there will still be problems. But at least employees will be trying to fix issues and serve customers.

How can you tell from the outside if people don't care? In the interview, ask questions like:

- How do you improve processes?
- What do customers love about what you do?
- What changes have you all struggled with over the past year?
- How do you keep up to speed on the newest technologies?

If the answers to these questions indicate apathy, then I'd avoid that employer. If you are already there, make plans to leave.

Another wart to avoid is nonsense. Unlike apathy, the definition of nonsense varies from person to person. Some people can't stand politics, while others can't stand shifting priorities. Some are frustrated by rigid hierarchies, while others need to know where they stand. I'm averse to politics, myself.

It will take you time to learn which nonsense disheartens you and which you can tolerate; try to distinguish the frustration you feel because you're being pushed to grow in a new environment from the sinking feeling in your gut telling you you're in the wrong job.

When talking to possible employers, find out what you can about their nonsense. To do so, ask questions such as:

- What's a typical day like?
- Who makes decisions about priorities? How are those decisions made?
- What kind of projects does this place shine at?
- What are the best and worst parts of your job?

No job is perfect, but by keeping an eye out for warts you can't tolerate, you'll be able to find an employer who matches what you need.

Sincerely,

Dan

Preparing for a recruiting event

Jeff Beard is a director of software development at Oracle Data Cloud. He would also like to acknowledge Caitlin Hickey and Mridula Natrajan for their help editing.

Dear new developer,

Preparing for a university job fair or similar recruiting event is very important if you want to make an impression that results in a phone screen.

A hiring manager and their recruiters receive an enormous number of contacts and resumes from a variety of channels so you have to be able to stand out from the crowd in a very short amount of time, often measured in seconds.

However, when you are at a recruiting event, you have a unique opportunity to make an impression since you will get to talk directly to a recruiter or even a hiring manager. So you need to be fully prepared to exploit that short window of opportunity.

Here are a few important things to prepare in order to make the most of that moment:

- Resume
- The introduction
- The conversation
- Appearance

Resume

A resume is something of a pitch deck that you use to get attention and tell your story. It's also a notepad and reminder for a recruiter or hiring manager to go back to in order to find you in the huge pile of resumes they collect—or, sadly, to figure out what goes into the recycle bin now vs. later (it's no joke: a desk covered with hundreds of resumes requires triage).

To begin with, make sure that you have complete basic information such as address, phone, email, GPA, and graduation date (for students) at the top of your resume.

There are a few important attributes that a hiring manager is looking for and that you want to show with your resume:

- Motivated

- Passionate

- Skilled

- Adaptable

- Collaborative

- Articulate

Since you are early in your career, you won't have as much work experience so you should make projects the centerpiece of your resume. In fact, even later in your career, a highly informative discussion can be had around projects that reveal the attributes noted earlier. For any project on your resume, you should be able to speak to:

- The purpose of the project

- Why it was important

- Did you work on a team

- How did the team self-organize

- How you overcame challenges

- What was the outcome

- Why you liked the project

Importantly, what a good hiring manager is looking for is intrinsic motivation. We want folks that are naturally excited about the domain they are looking to enter for their career.

So put your favorite project at the top of the list and drive the conversation to that project if you can. The person you are talking to needs to see what lights you up, and there is native passion for your favorite project that you need to let shine through. The project description should be brief and to the point, with a focus on the "what," "why," and the outcome. A project description doesn't need to be burdened with the tech used unless it adds to the overall narrative.

Projects don't have to be school class projects or work experience. They can be side hustles, open source, personal interest, or hackathon projects.

If you haven't done a lot of projects, take the initiative to find a couple of projects to work on. If you are in school or in your first job and it's not producing projects that engage you, seek them out or invent them yourself.

This will be reflected in your resume and will send a signal that you are curious and passionate about the domain and look beyond what you are doing day to day for interesting problems to solve.

One final bit of advice on resumes: Have more than one resume for different audiences. For example, if you are equally interested in DevOps and software development, craft two different resumes that highlight projects and work experience in each category. You can also optimize resumes for different industries to highlight aspects of your experience or interests that cast you in a good light for that market.

The introduction

The introduction is a critical face-to-face interaction that is your opportunity to form a connection with a potential hiring manager or recruiter. There is an incredibly short window of opportunity to impress the person, which means you need to say a few impactful words, delivered with confidence.

When you approach the company representative, reach out to shake hands while you say hello and start your introduction. People receive signals from a handshake so don't go soft and don't be aggressive. Just a firm, confident handshake will do the trick. Practice with friends.

I personally will listen for about a minute before I interrupt and direct the conversation to, say, the resume in a candidate's hand, but it's important to have a story that is concise, to the point, and well rehearsed.

The introduction should contain your name, your college program and graduation date (if appropriate), what you are passionate about, what role you are looking for, what your interest is in the company, and why you would be successful. It's a brief statement of intent and a value proposition signal. You should practice saying it out loud often enough that you can deliver it with a practiced confidence, energy, and restrained enthusiasm while looking the person straight in the eye.

Don't make assumptions about the person you are talking to; ask them what their role is at the company. If they are technical, this is an opportunity to signal your depth. If they are not, you can tailor the conversation accordingly.

Also don't launch into a description of every item on your resume; exercise restraint and stay focused on a concise introduction that will lead into a conversation.

Finally, like resumes, you can have more than one introduction crafted for different audiences.

The conversation

Your introduction will lead into a very short, general conversation which you also need to be prepared for. If the introduction is the hook, then this conversation is closing the deal on a phone screen. (Note you are not closing the deal on a job or an interview, that's later. You just want a second look which is what the phone screen is.)

You get it by handing the recruiter or hiring manager your resume to scan and ask their questions. Have a ready answer for everything on your resume including any questions about whether or not things went bad on a project or an obviously short tenure at one of your jobs.

You should also seek to align your interests with what the company does which requires research.

At most career fairs, there is a list of companies available ahead of time so you can research them and target the companies that do work that best aligns with your interests. If you aren't sure about what your passions are or it's hard to figure out what the company does, be prepared to put that out there right away. Some of the most awkward moments are when someone tries to improvise what they think my company does. Don't improvise, do the research. It's easy and pays dividends.

Just identify a few things that the company does to show interest and then ask about other things the company does and what market they operate in. What's important is that you show that you are interested and motivated enough to do the research. This also helps with the common question you may get: "why do you want to work for Willard's Widgets?" If you've done the research, you'll have a good idea of whether you can honestly say that whatever they do is super interesting and you'd love to help the company be successful.

Other questions you can ask are "what is the culture like?" and "tell me about an exciting initiative at the company," and as you wrap up the conversation, you could ask "when can I expect to hear back?"

To get extra credit, educate yourself on the industry that the company operates in. If you can speak intelligently about the major trends in a market and tie it to what a company does, you are instantly distinguished from your peers. Very few early-career candidates pay much attention to the business side of things, but it's important to understand the industry you work in, especially as you mature in your career.

Appearance

No need to wear a suit; it's not the norm for our industry except for executives (and even then there are a lot of hoodies and t-shirts in the wild). But don't wear pajamas with bunny slippers either. Casual clothes that are clean and not shredded, a folder full of printed resumes, and a cell phone are what you need when you step up to the table to confidently deliver that well-practiced introduction.

If you are comfortable with it, you can add something colorful, or otherwise visibly interesting or memorable, to your outfit that makes you stand out from the blue jeans/black leggings and t-shirt crowd. Don't be silly or obnoxious, just wear or add something visual and unique to your outfit or just make it more colorful in general. It provides something else for the hiring manager or recruiter to associate with a good conversation when they're digging through a pile of resumes, trying to decide who to call.

Finally, job fairs can be taxing so make sure you take breaks and have access to snacks and drinks to power you through the event and keep up your energy levels.

Sincerely,

Jeff

The surprising number of programmers who can't program

Dear new developer,

There's a class of interview problems which aren't difficult but exist to ensure someone who says they are a developer can actually write code. Yes, unfortunately, there are people who pretend they can develop software.

The canonical problem of this type is FizzBuzz. To solve this problem, you need to print the numbers from 1 to 100. If a number is divisible by 3, print "Fizz" instead of the number. If the number is divisible by 5, print "Buzz". If both are true, print "FizzBuzz".

This is not a complicated problem and can be answered quickly in an interview. It proves a candidate knows a language at a basic level. In Listing 9-1, you can see a FizzBuzz solution in Ruby:

Listing 9-1. *A solution to FizzBuzz*

```
(1..100).to_a.each do |n|
  if n % 3 == 0 && n % 5 == 0
    puts "FizzBuzz"
  elsif n % 3  == 0
    puts "Fizz"
  elsif n % 5 == 0
    puts "Buzz"
```

```
   else
     puts n
   end
end
```

There was some discussion about the efficacy of FizzBuzz in evaluating developers on Hacker News, an online community:[1]

> I've been working since the 90s and I never attempted to do FizzBuzz. Is it really relevant? Maybe to screen junior developers out of college?

Some comments were sobering:

> So, as someone who spends maybe 20% of their time hiring, it's still a very effective screen. You wouldn't believe how many people can't do it. People at big companies, respected places. It's surprising.

Over my career, I only can think of two colleagues who I believe couldn't program a solution to FizzBuzz. One in particular I remember basically having to excruciatingly lead him toward every solution. The project was structured such that I, a contractor, had to work with him. It was no fun, but I gritted my teeth and kept my eyes on the goal of delivering for the client.

As a new developer, realize that:

- You will be competing for jobs with people who can't program. Make sure you can.

- If you are one of the folks who can't program, fix that as soon as possible. Please. There are a lot of resources available online. Or seek a different type of technical position.

- There are ineffective programmers who still manage to find jobs as developers. You may end up working with them.

Make sure you practice programming. This book doesn't focus on the particulars of technical software development, but if you can't do the basic work of coding, you're going to have a tough time as a software engineer. Being a programmer who can't code is like being a professional baseball player who can't run. It doesn't matter how good someone is at catching a ball or hitting, if they can't run, they're going to have a hard time succeeding.

Sincerely,

Dan

---

[1]https://news.ycombinator.com/item?id=20673437

Start at a small consulting company

Dear new developer,

If you have a long-term goal for your career, work toward it. Whether the goal is mastering embedded programming, being a manager of a high-frequency trading team, or running a one-person web development contracting business, you can achieve it if you stay focused.

If the goal is your very first professional software development job, remember that to a large extent it is a matter of being at the right place at the right time. Keep applying and networking. Don't be too fussy about that first job.

If, however, you are looking to gain experience across technologies, domains, and businesses, work for a consulting company. If, in addition, you want to have an impact, work for a small one. This is where I started. I didn't really know what I was looking for, but I interviewed at large companies like HP. After college, I ended up getting an internship at a small web consultancy where I was one of the first 70 employees.

In this context, small means having between 10 and 75 employees. The lower limit of ten means the company is large enough to hire new developers and provide structure and support. Below that number, you'll have more autonomy, but other employees may be too busy to help you grow.

Seventy-five colleagues or fewer means that every hire matters. It's small enough that you'll have a relationship with everyone else at your company. Larger companies have places for people to hide and avoid real work. Small companies just don't have room for people not pulling their weight.

Consulting shops do a variety of work. If a project isn't working for you, you can shift to a different one. If that option isn't immediately available, you might have to gut it out for a few months. This is unpleasant, but a far cry from working on a product team you dislike for years.

Agencies are often hired for new projects, what is colloquially called "green field" development. This type of software engineering can be quite fun because there are fewer existing constraints on the system you are building.

As a consultant, you will get as much interaction with nontechnical folks as you desire; engineers with the ability and appetite for this are uncommon. You'll also learn how to build software to spec and on (or to be honest, near) budget.

On the flip side, smaller consulting companies tend to lack formal education programs. You must actively seek out mentorship, request conference attendance, and pursue assistance. These are good skills to develop, but if you aren't aware of the need, they may be overwhelming tasks piled on top of the actual work you were hired to do. Agency work can also be choppy, as projects start and stop based on the clients' needs.

Working at a small consulting company allows you to acquire a wide variety of technical and business experience. If you do a great job and keep track of people you work with, it can set your career up for the rest of your life. A majority of my jobs and contracts over my career have resulted from the people I met at that first consulting position, two decades ago.

Sincerely,

Dan

Potential vs. delivery

Dear new developer,

Early in your career, you are judged on potential. When you are young in your career, you don't have much of a track record, so there's not much else to judge you on.

Make sure you're exhibiting your capabilities to possible employers. Ask smart questions. Show you've learned your stuff. Say what you're going to do and then do it.

However, because potential matters for the early years, you can take career risks. Explore different areas of software development—technology, business size, or domain. Each time you shift, you'll bring useful experience, but mostly you'll be hired because of your capacity and willingness to learn. Companies must train you on their process and their technology stack and, as a new developer, they don't typically expect you to ship code on day one.

The more experienced you are, the less your potential matters, and the more you are assessed on your ability to deliver. The longer you are a developer, the more human capital, in the form of knowledge and experience, you possess. As a more senior developer, you are expected to deploy that capital. Your skill in doing so is assessed by examining your past accomplishments. The further along you are in your career, the more what you've done in the past is a harbinger of your future work.

Expect to demonstrate your experience during interviews. Outside endeavors such as contributing to open source are helpful. Don't reveal any work secrets in these conversations but expect to address the problems you've helped solve in general terms.

Periodically, or when you complete a project, take a few minutes to write down lessons you've learned. I blog, but a private journal works just as well. Then you can review this record before interviews. When you're asked "what is a difficult project you've worked on?", you'll have a cogent answer. Plus, you now have a personal retrospective; if you look back over past work and can't pinpoint any achievements, you may be in a job where you aren't progressing.

Even as an experienced developer, you won't necessarily be expected to commit code your first day. You'll need to learn how systems work. In fact, the bigger the company, the longer the spin-up period; I worked at a large software organization where people were surprised I expected to ship any code in the first week of my contract. But when you are an experienced developer, you need to slot in to your team and pick things up more quickly than a newer developer.

Once you're a senior developer, does that mean you cannot switch domains, tech stacks, or employer size? Absolutely not. But it does mean that you'll have a more difficult time doing so than a newer developer would. You'll need to convince hiring managers that your skills apply to the new position. A great book about making this type of switch is *What Color Is Your Parachute* by Richard Bolles.

The more experienced you are, the more constrained your choices become since you're judged on your past achievements. Take risks early.

Sincerely,

Dan

Maintain work-life balance

Dear new developer,

Preserve a firm boundary between your job and your life.

It's not easy to do. I've often felt the temptation to work work work, even though in most jobs I have not been paid overtime. Why?

- I wanted to "prove myself." Working extra hours is an easy way to be more productive, for a while.
- I was looking to be promoted or otherwise recognized.[2]
- I believed in the mission of my employer.
- Building stuff is fun.

Some extra work, some of the time, is okay. This is especially true if you are learning or enjoying it.

---

[2]This engineer did the grind and ended up getting the senior engineer title after a few years: "At night, even if I had went out with coworkers, I would go home and get back to work. I spent a lot of weekends staring at my computer screen while my friends frolicked (yes, I just said frolicked) at Dolores Park."—https://randallkanna.com/how-i-went-from-apprentice-to-senior-engineer-in-a-year-and-a-half/

However, make sure you set boundaries. Companies won't do that because the incentives are not there. A good manager will—I have seen managers force employees to take vacation. One of my best bosses said: "work is a marathon, not a sprint." As tempting as it is to overclock and work extra hours regularly, save this for special occasions.

Every project I've seen with a deadline has "crunch time." During such a time, I needed to work extra hours for a few weeks. Sometimes that was 45 hours in a week; other times it was 65 hours. But if you try to work like this year in and year out, eventually it will burn you out. You'll then have to take some time off and recuperate.

And even during crunch time, take care of yourself. I worked 96 hours one week to help save a project. The project launched, but I never got those hours back. A few years later, the project was shuttered. Would slipping a few weeks have had a material impact on my happiness? Yes, I would have been more of a human and less of a zombie. Would such slippage have had an impact on the long-term success of the project? No.

What can you do instead of working? So many options:

- Call up a friend.
- Find a hobby (that is not related to computers).
- Travel.
- Visit family.
- Get outside.
- Get inside.
- Read a book.
- Read a magazine.
- Volunteer.

How you spend your free time reflects your desires and options. More importantly, you must decide for yourself the balance you want between work and life. This ratio has changed for me over time—I used to be more interested in sitting down at the computer after work and cranking out some code or a blog post. Now I'm more likely to read to my child or meet a friend for a beer.

Once you've determined your boundaries, communicate them.

Be explicit by presenting choices to your manager: "I'd love to work on project X, but as of last week I understood the priority to be project Y, and I just don't have time to do both of them well. What should I do?" At job interviews, ask how you'd be expected to handle unplanned work. Yes, the issue is a bit scary, but employer expectations on this topic will have a large impact on your life. You also should ask about on-call expectations, as more and more companies are shifting this responsibility to developers.

You can communicate boundaries implicitly by not answering emails or chat messages outside of working hours. While doing so may not seem like a burden, it sends a message about when you are willing to work, which then may turn into an expectation. Leave Slack off your phone or configure its "do not disturb" mode.

Leave promptly at the end of the day. I'm not saying drop everything at 4:59— if you're in the middle of a conversation, finish it. But don't hang out till 6 or 8 p.m. regularly. Also, respect the work-life balance choices of your teammates. If they want to arrive early and leave early, good on them. If they must work from home periodically to deal with their obligations, adjust your expectations.

Expectation setting is even more important when you step into a leadership role. Many team members take cues from their leads and managers. Practicing this balance now ensures you will set a good example later.

Just as you need to manage your career because no one else will, you need to manage your work-life balance—no one else will. Employers and clients will only value your time as much as you do.

Sincerely,

Dan

Take this advice, or leave it

Rishi Malik has been a founder, manager, and engineer for over 15 years. You can reach him at www.rishim.com.

Hello new developer!

Right now, as I write this, it's Q1 2019. And there's a lot of advice you'll find out on the Internet. Much of it is good, some of it is bad, but the important thing to note is that what you read are all points of view from people—from that person to be specific. This letter is no different; this is just my view on what matters. Take it or leave it. In fact, that's the first point I want to make.

Tech is full of voices. Social media, popular blogs, and news sites amplify voices and feelings. This is an awesome thing, but remember that loud views aren't necessarily right.

What I mean is that you'll find points of view on everything. Developers have always loved flame wars and pointless battles (vi vs. emacs, tabs vs. spaces). Now it's "JavaScript developers aren't real engineers," or "If you can't code a binary search, you're a bad engineer."

Find yourself in all these voices. It's not easy, and it will take time. But work on what you value, and develop your skills to who you want to be. It's okay if you want to work by yourself on speeding up a search by .01 milliseconds. It's equally okay if you want to ship a single page app with a brilliant user experience. Listen to the voices when they help, and ignore them when they don't.

To help find yourself, focus on finding customers that value what you do. Most of the time, these customers are the people in the company you're working for. But if you want to do algorithms, find people who will value that work. If you want to work on networks, find companies who need that.

It sounds obvious, but it's an easy thing to miss when you're looking for a job and when you're evaluating comp, culture, benefits, and offices. It's also really hard to gauge from the outside of a company.

On that note, remember that the 2019 tech industry isn't how it will always be. Right now, the job market is stellar. I mean really stellar. In most big cities, you can find a job doing just about anything you want, most of the time within a few days.

This won't always be the case. It wasn't years ago, and everything comes in cycles. That's the second point. Be willing to do things you didn't think you wanted to. I worked on embedded systems when I started my career. I got into web technology not because I cared about it, but because it helped me get a job in a city where I wanted to live. Turned out to a prescient choice, and opened up tons of opportunities I wouldn't have had otherwise.

The tech choices come in cycles, but so does demand. I said before that the job market is stellar. But some of us old-timers have been through the downturns—when you're unemployed for 6 months because literally no one is hiring, when your choice is between a 50% pay cut or a 100% pay cut. Be wise; be smart. When it's a great time to be in tech, plan ahead for the times that are tough.

Finally, my last point is to remember that there is a world outside of tech. It's hard when you're in it to see that. When tech was smaller, and more insular, it was easier to remember that this is a job.

But now, tech is everywhere. Apps are everywhere. The Internet is everywhere. More people are writing code, building companies, and figuring things out. But, tech is not the entirety of life. Get outside of the tech zone, and connect with people who aren't in it. It will change how you think and how you develop code. And it provides a much needed break from the echo chamber that is tech.

Good luck, and have fun!

Rishi

Manage your career

Dear new developer,

You must manage your career. No one else will. This means:

1. Knowing your goals
2. Communicating those goals
3. Progressing toward them

Let's talk about each of these in turn.

Knowledge

Choosing goals is hard. We are lucky to live in a world with many opportunities. You can focus on one of a hundred different types of software development. There are other technology-related career paths such as product management, technology instruction, or engineering management. In all of these, software engineering skills will help you succeed.

In a world of opportunity, how should you choose? I pick an interest and follow it. This could be a language, a technique like debugging, or a broader skill like writing. Set a concrete goal such as being able to build a website using Ruby, manage a team, or write a book.

You can pick a broad scope, "I want to learn about DevOps," or a narrow focus: "I want to write CircleCI orbs that help deploy our software." Either is fine; you want a way to filter choices. It can even be something abstract like "I really want to work on an interesting problem." Even that will help you say yes or no to opportunities—whether jobs, projects, or new technologies to learn.

Once you possess certain fundamental skills, such as problem-solving, learning, and listening, you can change your career goals. For instance, I transitioned from being a web development contractor to a startup founder. I sacrificed earning potential and free time, but used many of the same skills.

Depending on your previous level of commitment and achievement, such change may not be an easy transition. You may pay a price in terms of compensation, status, or ego; you may have to spend free time learning new skills. But no decision is permanent. Pick what is interesting. Commit to it for six months or a year. Such a precondition will serve as another opportunity filter, helping you decide what to ignore.

Another way to choose which opportunity to pursue is to plan for a decade or more. You'll want to add milestones within that time period, as ten years is a long time. Technology changes quickly, so you'll want to be able to adjust your plan too. I don't have much experience with this process myself. I didn't do this when I was younger, preferring to follow my interests. When someone asks where I want to be in five or ten years, it's similar to where I am now—solving business problems with software. That or "retired"—but I can't say that in an interview.

Communication

After you have chosen a goal based on an interest, communicate your desires. If you don't talk about what you want, you will have a hard time getting it, unless you can accomplish it only through your own efforts. Even then, you'll get further sharing your ambitions. People want to help but need to know how.

So, discuss your desires with your manager, your communities, your friends, and your coworkers. Don't overshare, however; avoid mentioning the goal every day.

If you've talked about your ambitions with your manager and they've provided opportunities for you to work toward them, let them know how you've taken advantage. If your boss explains there's no chance for you to work on that interest in your current position, do some research on your own time. Share that research and explain how you achieving the goal will benefit the company.

The longer you are at a company and the better the work you do, the more latitude you will have. Managers want to keep employees who deliver quality work happy. The alternative is often hiring someone new because an unhappy employee left.

For example, if you are a web developer and want to be a database administrator, volunteer for database projects. Mention this goal to your manager at your one on ones. If there is a database team at your company, ask if you can meet with them regularly. Working toward this goal doesn't mean you can skip out on the web development work for which you are paid. Instead, you can tweak your work environment toward your interests. Good companies want to see their employees grow.

Progress

You can't simply communicate your desires, you have to act on them. Again, if you are that web developer hoping to become a database administrator, present on databases at a meetup. Heck, even attending a database meetup is progress. Run a brown bag lunch on databases at your company or read a book about the technology. Study for a certification. Apply what you learn to your current duties.

Take note of adjacent areas that pique your interest. These could be future topics to investigate.

Sometimes you can't make progress at your current employer. Maybe the opportunity isn't there. Maybe the company really needs you in your current position, and you don't have time for anything other than your expected duties.

You may have to switch jobs. That's okay. Don't burn any bridges, but when it is time to move on, leave. Find a new job with your skills and knowledge, but don't forget to communicate your ambitions during the interview process. Give notice to your current employer and head off to a new adventure.

What's the alternative? Floating through your career, buffeted from position to position with no plan, or worse, moving from one job you're afraid to lose to another.

That doesn't sound like much fun.

Sincerely,

Dan

Know your runway

Dear new developer,

When you are considering a big career jump, whether to a startup, a sabbatical, or further schooling, calculate your runway, which is how much time you have at your current level of spending before you have no money. Any time when your expenses will exceed your income, you need to know this. To figure this out, determine your current savings and your monthly net outflow: expenses minus any income not related to the job you are going to give up. Dividing your savings by your outflow gives you the months of runway you have. At the end of your runway, you will have no money; that makes living difficult.

No matter what you are considering, it's better to know this number ahead of time, rather than run off the edge of a financial cliff.

Calculate runway once a month. Also, think about how long it would take to get a new job. This will be a guess, but you can ask folks with similar experience who have found jobs how long it took. Before you transition, decide on the number of months of runway which will trigger a job search. For instance, if you begin with six months of runway, you may set a trigger at two months. If you reach that level of runway, seek other sources of income.

Whatever you do, get a job before you need to. Desperation makes interviews even harder than they already are. You may end up accepting an ill-fitting job; this sets you up for future stress. If benefits aren't important, consider contracting as a stopgap to allow a more relaxed interview process while at the same time lessening your financial bleeding.

If you have six months of runway, but the jump is expected to take longer, you have some hard choices. You can try to pursue the opportunity part time while you have a full-time job. You can quit or pause your startup or education midstream. You can try to increase your income, by moonlighting or joining the gig economy. You can decrease your expenses by moving to a less expensive house or cutting other spending.

Decreasing expenses is what you have the most control over, but it can be tough to do. However, other options are distracting, so cutting your spending is my recommendation, unless you are cutting expenses to the point that you are hungry all the time.

Whew. Sounds stressful. Why would you ever put yourself in a situation where you had to make these kinds of choices?

Spending savings for a career transition is an investment in yourself. When I joined a startup as a cofounder, I leveled up my skills in DevOps, customer empathy, community building, and product management. When I took a sabbatical, I learned how much I loved building software—I remember sitting in an Internet café reading an article about RDF, an XML technology that was the shiny new thing at the time.

Activities that draw down your savings lead to new opportunities and valuable personal knowledge. Just keep in mind how long you can afford such an investment so you aren't unpleasantly surprised.

Sincerely,

Dan

How to manage one on ones

Dear new developer,

Hopefully, you'll work at a place where you'll have regular one-on-one meetings with your manager. In addition to serving as a communication channel, such meetings strengthen the relationship.

One on ones tend to be 30–60 minutes in duration and are scheduled regularly, either weekly, biweekly, or monthly. If you are meeting face to face, you can have them in the office, but going for a walk or out to lunch is a great way to mix it up. If you are using video chat, it's best to have a great Internet connection, a quiet space, and video turned on. There are nuances you can only pick up from someone's facial expression.

These meetings allow you to easily give and receive feedback. If the only time you meet with your manager is when you've screwed up or when a raise is on the line, you'll dread feedback.

A regular one on one also helps both parties get to know each other. This rapport helps during stressful times. I had a meeting with a manager who pointed out how I had made a pretty big mistake. It was a hard conversation, but easier than it might have been because we'd gotten to know each other.

As a new developer, you might not have a scheduled one on one, if that isn't typical at your employer. If you don't, ask for a regular meeting with your supervisor. Suggest a monthly 30-minute meeting, which shouldn't be too hard to find time for. Emphasize how the meeting will help both the company and your supervisor by offering one or more of these reasons for the meeting:

- I want to understand where we are heading so I can know what to learn.

- I want to know how I can best help you and the company.

- I would like to understand your priorities better.

Framing it in this manner illustrates the value of the meeting, but in my experience, the agenda of a one on one should be owned by the employee. That doesn't mean that the manager never brings discussion items, but rather that the direction of the one on one should be determined by the employee.

Set up the meetings at a time that works for both parties. Be cognizant of each other's schedule; does someone like to get up early or work late? Are you in the same time zone? Scheduling these meetings back to back can make it easier for a manager. Slotting them outside of contiguous "in the zone" time blocks can make sure that you can get work done.

The meeting must happen regularly. They don't have to take the entire scheduled duration, but the manager should never cancel them and only rarely reschedule them. If they must be shifted, find a new time promptly. This meeting is important for you as a new developer. If your manager is stretched too thin or is for whatever reason not treating the one on one as an important meeting, suggest decreasing the frequency. Realize that this is a signal from your boss that they can't or don't prioritize interactions with you. However, a meeting that actually happens once a month is better than a weekly meeting that is constantly cancelled.

What can you do if your boss isn't interested? Think about other ways to get feedback, either from other team members or in an asynchronous format from your manager. You could, for example, send him or her a weekly status report. Your manager's guidance is critical for your early career growth, and if they can't carve time out for you, you may want to seek a new position.

When you have a one on one scheduled, make the most out of it. Come with your agenda. I use a shared document in reverse chronological order, with notes about the current meeting at the top. Share this with your manager. Over the time between your meetings, add items you want to discuss to this document; you might include relevant questions like these:

- How should I have handled situation ABC?
- I'd like to learn more about NoSQL databases; what are the opportunities?
- I'm struggling with <problem>, do you have any suggestions?
- What are the challenges you see facing our team during project YYY?
- I heard a rumor that we're opening a London office; is there anything you can tell me about that?

In general, topics should be professional challenges, discussions, or opportunities. Chitchat about what you did over the weekend is a good social lubricant, but I've found it can go awry. But if that's what you want to discuss, and you feel that will strengthen the relationship, well, it's your meeting. As a manager, I've found that discussing reports' personal hobbies can lead to good conversations and a stronger rapport. As an individual contributor, I've also struggled with managers who would occasionally hijack a one on one with their own worries and prevent me from bringing up my issues. If that happens, gently try to bring the meeting's focus back to your concerns.

I like to record action items for myself and my manager in the document. Sometimes the action item is as simple as "bring this topic up again in three months." When the next one on one happens, I can see what we discussed last time; everyone can see if there has been any progress. This document is also great for preparing for your performance review, sharing with a new supervisor, or even just reviewing occasionally to gain perspective.

I have learned one on ones are the right place for me to ask for what I want. It's awkward, because I'm a people pleaser, but if I don't ask for what I want from my supervisor, how will he or she know? That doesn't mean I can ask for the moon, but if I see interesting opportunities in areas adjacent to my current work, I ask if I can take advantage of them.

For example, if you run across products you think would make everyone's lives easier, ask if you can investigate them. If you see a interesting conference, ask if you can attend. I remember at my first job I was interested in learning about database administration. I asked my supervisor about doing an internal internship in that group, and they allowed me.

What is said in a one on one should be kept private, unless sharing it is discussed and both parties agree. Keep the agenda document between the two of you. Of course, there are exceptions, such as illegal activities, and Roy Rappaport does a great job of breaking down the alternatives in his article, "The 1-on-1 Disclosure Framework."[3]

It's worth acknowledging that there's a power differential in every one on one meeting. The manager has a lot of influence on the employee's role, salary, and continued employment. The employee, on the other hand, does not affect the manager's job directly. Trust is imperative, and if it isn't present, no amount of chitchat will help.

If you can't trust your manager to do right by you, try building that trust with smaller asks during the one on ones. If those go nowhere, my advice is to find a new job. A job where you can't rely on your boss is not a pleasant job.

The one-on-one meeting isn't about being buddies or friends, but rather about building your professional relationship with your supervisor. This will help both parties thrive and work toward company goals.

Sincerely,

Dan

Write a brag document

Dear new developer,

You will encounter good managers and bad managers in your career. One common thread is that all managers are busy—busy with meetings, busy coordinating with other teams, busy putting out fires, busy helping. Busy busy busy.

But your manager influences your current and future job opportunities. Promotions, compensation increases, and title changes all are earned by you, but controlled by a manager or a system to which the manager is a gatekeeper. A good manager will want you to be challenged and grow and learn.

However.

The only person who really cares, deeply and truly, about your career is you— well, maybe your mother too.

You can help your manager help you by letting them know your accomplishments. This may feel like an undue burden. You may think: "surely my manager can keep track of what I've accomplished." And supervisors may know some of the stuff you've done, some of the time.

---

[3]https://medium.com/@royrapoport/the-1-on-1-disclosure-framework-bec6118402ce

But what you want is to show them everything you're proud of. This lets them know what a great team member you are. It also gives them ammunition to fight for resources you deserve: pay raises, interesting projects, and learning opportunities.

One place to share your achievements is your LinkedIn profile. However, this will be limited because you shouldn't share too much detail or reveal company secrets. It is a good place to document projects and successes at a high level.

You should also maintain a brag document. Julia Evans has a great post on how to write one.[4] This document should highlight all the work you've done in a thorough but easy-to-read form. This will help you track progress and projects too. It also helps inform your manager. It can be far more detailed than LinkedIn since it is private. Julia suggests threading together your accomplishments into a bigger story:

> In addition to just listing accomplishments, in your brag document you can write the narrative explaining the big picture of your work. Have you been really focused on security? On building your product skills & having really good relationships with your users? On building a strong culture of code review on the team?

You can pull this document out when your performance review rolls around. When combined with your cumulative one on one agendas, you should have a good idea of your successes and challenges. Having such a record of your accomplishments which you can share with your busy manager will help them help you.

Sincerely,

Dan

Be adaptable and authentic

Morgan Whaley is a senior prototype architect at Charter Communications.

Dear new developer,

Honestly, my #1 piece of career or technical advice to new developers is

Be adaptable and authentic.

I don't think there is any one magic bullet to helping someone "break into" a job, or business, or new city. Humans are all different, and the beauty of diversity in industry and environments is when everyone truly brings

---

[4]https://jvns.ca/blog/brag-documents/

themselves and overrides the homogenization that we accuse modern cities and tech of becoming.

If something isn't working, there's "no harm, no foul" in changing approaches, or taking a break, or simply admitting something isn't working.

I see a lot of people who treat that first job like it's a task they gotta beat into submission, and they tie so much self-worth to it, which is completely understandable, but the more you resist a situation and don't remain open to possibilities, the more you are going to run into brick walls.

Morgan

PS Also, LEAVE YOUR HOUSE AND GO TALK TO PEOPLE FACE TO FACE OH MY GOD, PLEASE IT'LL BE OK.

Are you ready to work remotely?

Dear new developer,

Remote work is great. You avoid commutes, have control over your work environment, and save money on lunches. However, it has its downsides. You need a fast Internet connection, iron discipline, and the ability to work through communication obstacles. You also must be okay with solitude.

My desire to work remotely has changed over my career. For my first job, there's no way I would have been happy working out of my house. I enjoyed the collaboration, the camaraderie, and the office full of interesting people.

There is a fundamental difference between being physically present and being on a video call, phone call, or screenshare. Anyone who has tried to walk a parent through resetting their router knows that. If you are a new developer in a 100% remote work environment, ask if there are opportunities for in-person interaction. When I once joined a company as a remote employee, I spent the first week working from corporate headquarters and made trips there every month or so. This helped me build a relationship with other employees and made it easier for me to know who to ask for help when I needed it.

A 100% remote job is different from "work from home once a week" or "work from home when you need to." Fully remote work requires a different workflow and communication strategy. Some people are never going to want to work from home all the time due to these differences, and that's okay.

Here is a one-question test for anyone considering remote work. You can ask yourself this, and if the answer is yes, a remote position will work well for you. If the answer is no, then you'd be happier on-site.

That question is *"Are you comfortable asking a dumb question?"*

You must ask questions that appear dumb when you get up to speed in any new company or project. Developers of all levels do this. These questions aren't actually dumb, but because you don't have context, they can feel dumb. Usually, there are two levels of queries. The first is "who can help with this?"; the second is asking the actual question to the appropriate employee. You can shortcut this by asking the question in a public chat or meeting, but this may be even more intimidating.

In a remote company, you must accept that you are interrupting people by asking such questions. Whereas on-site you can see if someone is hunched over their computer with deep focus, in a remote situation you can't see other employees' nonverbal cues. You don't know if you're asking them when they're on a break or heads down doing deep work. Chat system statuses can provide some insight but aren't always accurate and don't convey the same level of information as you'd get walking by someone's desk.

But you'll need answers, so you'll have to interrupt. The alternative is trying to figure it out yourself, which will often waste time. So be prepared to ask this type of question often.

If that thought of asking these questions makes you uncomfortable, congrats, you're human.

But if it makes you want to run away and hide, then perhaps you aren't ready for remote work. Maybe you need a bit more guidance than will be available in such a position. If you are interested in the flexibility and freedom of 100% remote work, wait a few years until you've internalized the fact that asking dumb questions is part of the learning process at any job.

Sincerely,

Dan

How to go through a layoff

Dear new developer,

At some point in your career, you might get laid off. I did.

I've also been through a company layoff where I kept my job. It stunk. It felt like I was sticking around on a slowly sinking ship. I also had survivor's guilt; good teammates had been let go. Layoffs aren't fun for anyone involved.

But, before I write any more about being laid off, I want to be clear. I am not a lawyer. *Please don't take this as legal advice.*

If you are the one being let go, it's going to be hard.

You get called in for the meeting. Your boss is there. Someone from HR is there. They tell you the company has decided to part ways—with you.

Your heart sinks. You are handed a big fat packet of paper, full of information about benefits, unemployment, and legal obligations. The HR person runs through it and asks if you have any questions. You feel dazed.

Take a deep breath. Realize that no matter how crushing this feels right now, two things are true:

- This isn't personal.
- You'll get through this.

It's hard not to feel wounded when you are laid off. After all, you've spent most of your waking weekday hours supporting this company and its mission. But the truth is that organizations have to make hard choices. Sometimes employees have to be let go to help the company survive. I've seen managers agonize over these decisions. Now, it's not harder for the managers than it is for the laid off workers—the managers still have their jobs after all—but it's no walk in the park for them.

Back to the meeting. Ask any questions you have. Here are some important ones:

- By when do I have to sign this packet of documents?
- Is there a severance, and if so, how much?
- What about other funds that are mine, such as a 401k, FSA, or HSA?
- How can I say goodbye to my teammates?
- What about other property which belongs to the company, such as a laptop, books, or equipment? How can I get that back to the company?
- Who at the company should I contact if I have other questions?

Don't be unprofessional.

Don't get mad.

Don't try to get your job back (it's gone, sorry!).

Don't agree to anything other than reviewing the paperwork.

Make sure they have your personal email for further communication. By the way, if the company has their act together, you won't have access to your work accounts after the meeting.

You may ask why you are being let go. Don't be surprised if you don't get a satisfactory answer.

Say goodbye to your teammates. Emails or LinkedIn messages are good options. Write a quick note to your former coworkers stating that you enjoyed working with them. Express regret that you're leaving, but even if you are angry, don't badmouth anyone. Such a tone only reflects poorly on you.

After the meeting, take notes on what happened. Use your own computer or notebook. Writing down your experience will help make sure you understood everything that happened. If you want, add some details about anything leading up to the layoff. Some things might have been obvious warning signs—at one company, I kept trying to schedule a time to visit the home office, and it kept getting put off.

Before you sign any legal documents, it's a good idea to run the agreements by an employment lawyer. If you don't know a lawyer, ask for a referral from a friend. Yes, such a review will cost a lot of money as lawyers charge hundreds of dollars an hour, but they've seen such contracts before and are legally obligated to do right by you. The lawyers who wrote up the agreements are obligated to look out for the company. Your lawyer should be able to advise you on topics like noncompetes and nondisparagement agreements.

At this point, it's "just business," so protect yourself. Ask the lawyer for their advice. Also make clear your budget and timeline; I've never had a lawyer push back if I said "I only have $1000 for this. Please let me know if you're getting close to that number." The bill might hurt, but don't forget that they will save you from making expensive mistakes like signing away your right to work for a competitor.

There may be some back and forth with the company over the agreements. Depending on the situation, you may have more leverage, but your end goal should be to quickly wrap up the separation in a way that feels like you're not being taken advantage of. After the review by your lawyer and perhaps an exchange or two with the company, you can sign the agreement. Or you may not, in which case you can ask the lawyer what your other options are.

Either way, take some time to grieve, even if you can only afford a day. When I was laid off, I took a long afternoon walk which helped me process the event. Even if the company or job wasn't a perfect fit, being laid off hurts.

Then, roll up your sleeves and start looking for a new opportunity. Is it time to try contracting? Maybe something else that is risky? Or to reach out to your network and see what is available?

A layoff feels like a defeat. But you'll get through it.

Sincerely,

Dan

Use LinkedIn

Dear new developer,

Set up a LinkedIn profile and keep it up to date. It is basically a public resume. Yes, a GitHub or other code repository profile is useful as well, but you might not always have time to keep that code polished—text is easier. Once every year, update your profile with what you've accomplished. Hiring managers will often look at it, and you want to impress them.

Keep track of former colleagues or others you meet in a professional context using LinkedIn. If you meet people at jobs, conferences, or meetups, ask if you may connect to them. Folks have different thresholds—some people connect to anyone, others want to meet you, and some won't connect unless they have worked with you. It doesn't hurt to ask; don't be offended if someone says no thanks or doesn't accept the invite once you send it. My personal threshold is "have I met you in person or engaged with you online?" My connections are of varying strength—some connections I'd hire at the drop of a hat; others I met only once.

In the same way, determine your connection criteria. Do you want to connect to everyone? Only people you've talked to? A friend asked for an intro to a LinkedIn connection recently, and I couldn't provide one because the connection wasn't someone I really knew. Is it even useful for me to have that person in my LinkedIn network? Probably not, which means I should reconsider my threshold.

If you do end up sending requests to people you've met only briefly, always include a note. This differentiates you from the drive-by connector. It can be as simple as stating where you met them: "It was nice to meet you last week at the Boulder Ruby meetup. I'd like to connect with you."

Depending on your skill set and the strength of the job market, you'll probably be contacted by recruiters on LinkedIn. Such recruiters tend to be low-value keyword matchers. But you never know, someone might be able to place you in a job. If you do talk to a recruiter, be honest about your desires. Take what they say with a grain of salt because they are trying to sell you on the position. While you are having the conversation, ask them about their view of the job market, salary ranges for people with your experience, and good skills to learn. If they aren't willing to or cannot share such information, they won't be much good to work with. Whatever you decide, treat the recruiters with professionalism; please don't troll them.

LinkedIn is an address book which someone else keeps up to date. When you are looking for a job, examine your connections' companies, review posted jobs, and then ask if your connection can introduce you. Make it easy for them by writing up a note explaining why the company is awesome, why you are awesome, and why you want to work for them. A warm intro is more likely to lead to a conversation and interview than submitting a resume via a website. If you have a job, do the same for others who reach out for this kind of help.

LinkedIn is a powerful professional tool. It can help you find a job, keep in touch with former colleagues, and assist other people.

Sincerely,

Dan

Contracting

Dear new developer,

You have a portable skill set; every company needs software, just like everyone needs accountants. You have a "means of production" that only costs a few thousand dollars: your laptop. You can learn new skills for the low cost of an Internet connection and your time. Especially after you have a few years of experience, you are in demand.

Please take a chance during the first decade of your career and try contracting.

Why? I like contracting because it is similar to applying for a job every few months. Whoa, who likes applying for a job? The hiring process for contractors is easier than interviewing for a full-time position because contractors are easier to let go. Having to regularly find and engage with hiring managers and clients means you must keep your skills sharp and your ear to the ground for opportunities. Honing these skills for a few years means that if and when you become an employee again, job hunting won't be anywhere near as scary. Who knows, you might even "go feral," as a friend of mine says, and never want to be a full-time employee again.

You'll also strengthen your network because you'll run across opportunities that aren't a fit for you but might be for a former colleague. Share those and I guarantee former coworkers will remember you fondly. When you are contracting, depending on the arrangement, you may be paid for every hour you work. The rate is typically higher than it would be if you were a full-time employee. Contracting can be very lucrative.

There are two paths to contracting. You can work with an agency; they will place you at their clients. The other option is contracting directly with clients.

The first is easier. The agency finds the work, sorts out what kind of developers are needed, and sends you to the client. You'll be paid by the agency, typically by the hour. You'll have the chance to experience many different organizational structures and technologies, without doing anything other than showing up. Depending on the agency, you may be able to switch between clients. The downsides of working through an agency are that you'll receive a lower hourly rate than you would if you contracted directly—basically, you're paying for them to take care of sales and accounting.

Contracting directly with clients is more difficult. If you do this, you'll learn skills beyond software development: sales, customer support, marketing, invoicing, and chasing payments. All these are powerful additions to your toolkit. If nothing else, they'll give you an appreciation for everyone who works at a software company who isn't an engineer, because when you contract directly with clients, you perform all those job functions. Getting such a business running will take longer than calling an agency, passing their interview, and getting placed at a client. But you'll have a lot more control over the clients you work with and more income.

I've met plenty of people making less money as a direct to client contractor than as an employee. They're working harder too. Why? They don't raise their rates, and they work for cheap clients—clients who don't value their time. Fire bad clients by finding new ones and then ceasing to work for those who don't treat you right. To do this, you must be always on the lookout for new prospective customers.

Depending on the market you are in, you may spend as much as 50% of your time on non-billable work, which is often seeking new opportunities. Make sure your rate reflects this. Writing blog posts, contacting past clients, and being engaged in local communities such as the chamber of commerce, meetups, or a local Slack workspace all will help you when your current contract is over.

You must raise your rates every time you have a new client until prospective clients are saying you charge too much. You can also raise rates of your existing clients on a yearly cadence. How do you find out how much to charge? I've found most contractors are happy to chat rates, especially over lunch. If you're too busy, you are pricing your labor too low.

Even if you want to be a full-time employee for the rest of your career, a stint as a contractor introduces you to new ideas, teaches you new skills, and will give you an appreciation for the work of nonengineering colleagues.

Sincerely,

Dan

Engineering management

Dear new developer,

As a new engineer, you're probably a few years away from thinking about the challenges of engineering management—but perhaps not. If you join a startup rocketship, you may be managing people in months. Moving into management is a common career path for a developer as they gain experience.

However, management is an entirely new job. A pattern I've seen again and again is a developer being hired, sticking around, and becoming more experienced on a team. More responsibility is handed to him or her. They meet with clients or other representatives of the business. They are responsible for technical delivery of a product. They mentor other team members on "how things are done around here." Eventually, someone in authority asks if they would like to be promoted to an engineering manager position—or worse, doesn't even formally ask, just heaps on the responsibility with no conversation.

If this happens to you, new developer, beware. The difference between software development and engineering management is like the difference between American football and soccer. Familiarity with one will help you understand the other. They both are about scoring points and moving a ball around. But at the end of the day, they are fundamentally different. If you move from software development to engineering management, prepare to be a novice again.

The skills that make you a great developer won't make you a great manager. Developers solve problems; managers help others solve problems. Developers focus; managers communicate. Developers code; managers listen and plan. It's not an entirely disjoint union, but if you take this step, know that you'll be starting over and you'll have a lot to learn.

Here are some other tips when it comes to engineering management:

- You should have your hands in the code so you can follow along, but you must stay out of the critical path of software delivery.

- People closest to the code should make technical decisions. Hint—that is not you.

- Enabling teams to do great work is your new problem space.

- You should not do the fun technical stuff at work, except during hackathons.

Being an engineering manager isn't a terminal choice. You can shift back and forth between engineering management and a senior individual contributor role. This is a potent combination because you will understand technical details enough to work on the code, but you also know how to navigate an organization to get things done. Charity Majors outlined this option in her blog post, "Engineering Management: The Pendulum Or The Ladder."[5] She also covers another choice, "climbing the ladder," which leads to ever more meetings and responsibilities. Charity doesn't mince words when it comes to these choices:

---

[5]https://charity.wtf/2019/01/04/engineering-management-the-pendulum-or-the-ladder/

One warning: Your company may be great, but it doesn't exist for your benefit. You and only you can decide what your needs are and advocate for them. Remember that next time your boss tries to guilt you into staying on as manager because you're so badly needed, when you can feel your skills getting rusty and your effectiveness dwindling. You owe it to yourself to figure out what makes you happy and build a portfolio of experiences that liberate you to do what you love. Don't sacrifice your happiness at the altar of any company. There are always other companies.

I don't tell you this now, new developer, because I want to scare you away from management. I have been an engineering leader and enjoyed it. You have autonomy, you can help fix problems you see in your organization, and you get to recruit and help people grow into the best developers that they can be. But it's a step away from some of the joyful parts of software development—building things, solving hard technical problems, and being a doer. Make this choice with your eyes open.

Sincerely,

Dan

Someday, you won't want to code for a living

Dear new developer,

I remember my first full-time software engineering job. I was able to work on a great team and interesting problems. I regularly got into "flow," that magical state where time passes unnoticed and much code is written. I was paid well. They had free snacks.

I remember going into my manager's office and chatting with him. He seemed a bit stressed. He was constantly interrupted. He had lots of meetings. He seemed to want to code but didn't have time. I asked him once why he hadn't remained an engineer. Why would he leave a really fun job for management? He looked at me with a knowing smile and said something like "one day, you'll understand."

I don't code for a living now. Oh, sure, I write some code. And it still gets me into a state of flow. I enjoy it. But when I am coding, I have limited influence. As I grow older, I grow more impatient to effect change in the world. The best way to do so is to have more leverage.

Becoming a manager is one way to gain that, but not the only way. These activities let you influence or inform more people than you might as a hands-on-keyboard coder:

- Writing
- Project management

- Product management
- Speaking
- Starting a business
- Mentoring
- Leading a team
- Managing
- Teaching
- Architecting
- Consulting

Most of these involve communicating about software engineering, but coding is not the primary work output. Instead, the emphasis is on a product, knowledge sharing, or team alignment.

There are also ways to get leverage which keep your hands firmly enmeshed in code:

- Working on large systems with a lot of users
- Working on popular open source libraries

If either of those options floats your boat and you want to keep coding, pursue them. I don't like the first because I don't really enjoy the bureaucracy of big companies. I am not a fan of the second because I don't really enjoy working for free.

By the way, no one says you must pursue leverage. I'm just saying you probably will. I've seen it happen in many companies and with many individuals. Part of it might be that more leverage typically means a higher salary.

Your salary will be higher because you provide more value. With a higher leverage position, the company benefits in ways beyond the software you write. For example, if you're a team lead, the communication you have with stakeholders to ensure the software will meet their needs on their schedule is quite valuable.

A career is long. My guess is that one day you won't want to *only* code for a living. Enjoy it now but keep your eyes open and think about other options which might be of interest.

Sincerely,

Dan

In conclusion

I remember when I turned 25. I was glum. A work colleague asked what was wrong. I explained I'd already been through 25% of my life and hadn't achieved much. He laughed and said that I'd really only been through five years of adulthood and that I'd likely work another seven half decades, so in reality I wasn't that far into my career.

As I look back, having worked through a few more half decades, what I can do and what I'm interested in have both changed. While I haven't had a long-term plan, I've taken advantage of some breaks. New challenges have arisen. Some I've succeeded at. At others I've failed.

Your career is long. You need to manage it, whether that is tactically asking for what you need during a one on one, working toward larger career goals, or simply keeping in touch with former colleagues on LinkedIn.

Community

I joined a Ruby meetup a few years ago because I was working with Ruby on Rails, a web technology framework. I wanted to learn more about it and meet fellow practitioners. After a few months, I'd learned a lot, but better, I'd met interesting people. It was a sacrifice of a night every month, but it was worth it.

A few years after I joined, I volunteered to find speakers for this meetup, which gave me the opportunity to help the meetup organizers and reach out to prominent people in the Ruby community. At present, I don't work with Ruby very much anymore, but I still attend and help because I love the network I've built, the education I receive, and the friends I've made. Every month we get together. I see familiar faces and new ones too.

Meetups are prevalent in the technology world. Other vocations have professional organizations and events, but rarely are they as volunteer driven, frequent, and diverse as technology meetups. Software development is so sprawling and evolves so quickly that developers need to self-educate to maintain their edge. But the profession is so young that, unlike medical doctors or lawyers, there are fewer institutions which provide education, let alone licensure.

There are of course ways to build networks other than joining a meetup. You can find community online, from your school, or from your work. Where you find it is less important than that *you find one*. Community members help you learn, provide contextual advice, and cheer you on when you succeed.

But wait, there's more!

More than half of the jobs and contracts I've had over my two decade career resulted from introductions by former colleagues or people I'd met in a

© Dan Moore 2020
D. Moore, *Letters to a New Developer*, https://doi.org/10.1007/978-1-4842-6074-6_10

professional setting. Working with people you know makes everything easier. It is easier to get an interview, easier to be hired, and easier to understand team dynamics and be productive. Jobs are hard enough; having a network is like a cheat code.

You can also lend a hand to community members. You can help them when they need advice, or have something to publicize, or need to find a job.

Finding "your people" isn't just a fun way to learn and help others; it will help you as well.

Meetups

Dear new developer,

You are probably overwhelmed right now. There is a lot on your plate, and you are probably just trying to keep up with your job duties. Or maybe you are seeking employment, which feels like a high-stakes full-time endeavor.

I hate to do this, but I am going to ask you for some extracurricular time.

Join a technology meetup. Go to www.meetup.com and search for one in your area, focused on a technology you want to learn. Sign up and attend the next one. If there is no meetup in the area, search for one that is virtual.

When you are at this meetup, you might have a hard time chatting with people—I know I do! I find the best way to engage with people is to be interested in what they have to say. Show up 15 minutes early. Find someone standing alone; walk up to them and introduce yourself. Then ask what brings them to the meetup and what they are working on. Starting these conversations will be awkward at first, but, like coding, it gets easier the more you do it.

If it is a virtual meetup, conversations are harder. Instead, you might want to see if there is a Slack channel or Twitter hashtag for asynchronous communication. Mention you went to the meetup and start a conversation around the topic of the presentation.

Either way, enjoy the talks. You'll learn something. You should spend some of your precious free time at a meetup because:

- It will expose you to new ideas that you can bring to your job.

- It will allow you to have professional conversations with low stakes. For example, it is generally easier to admit ignorance to a new friend than to your boss.

- It will allow you to practice talking to new people; you'll have at least the topic of the meetup in common.

- You can make friends and acquaintances in your industry.
- When you are ready to hunt for a new job, you will have a network outside of your coworkers.
- You will meet cool people.
- You will learn about new concepts and projects.

You may, in time, choose to help organize or speak at a meetup. These activities will also help your career. But if all you do is attend a meetup regularly, you will still come out ahead.

Please, go sign up for a meetup today.

Sincerely,

Dan

Conversational hooks

Dear new developer,

It's hard to build community if you can't talk to people. I often feel awkward around folks I don't know. Over the years, I have learned how to be less stiff. My main technique is to both give and ask for a "hook" in any conversation I start.

Here's a typical "networking" conversation I've had:

Dan: "Hi, I'm Dan."

Rohana: "Hi, I'm Rohana."

Dan: "Where do you work?"

Rohana: "I work at Company X. Where do you work?"

Dan: "Company Y."

\<crickets\>

So awkward. I am cringing just reading this. Typically, at this point, both Dan and Rohana look around for someone else to talk to so they can escape the silence.

Compare that with this conversation:

Dan: "Hi, I'm Dan."

Rohana: "Hi, I'm Rohana."

Dan: "Where do you work?"

Rohana: "I work at Company X. Where do you work?"

Dan: "Company Y. We recently launched website Z and are evaluating technology ABC. What has your company recently rolled out?"

New developer, do you see the difference? In the second conversation, Dan has provided Rohana with two avenues for conversation—she can either focus on Dan and ask about technology ABC or website Z or can answer Dan's question about Company X. She can decide where to take the conversation, but Dan has offered up some possible directions. Without the hooks, Rohana might not have known that Dan had exposure to technology ABC. But with them, she may have questions to ask or opinions to share. In any event, the dreadful silence is avoided.

I've also found that most people love to talk about themselves. I do. The hook provides concrete opportunities for Rohana to talk about herself or her employer. Everyone, every single person, has an interesting, educational story to tell.

Starting a conversation with a stranger is the first step to getting to know them. That can help you with whatever you seek, whether hiring a team member, making a sale, finding a mentor, or learning the warts of a new technology.

Don't be transactional, however. Have you ever been approached by someone and as soon as they found out you couldn't help them, they exited the conversation? It feels icky. You don't have to be everyone's best friend but work to find something interesting about anyone you are talking to.

Having a professional relationship with people outside your company can help your career directly. For example, it's rare that you find a new job via your current coworkers—they probably want you to stick around. This is where networking events and meetups shine. Learning to provide a conversational hook made such events far more pleasant.

Sincerely,

Dan

Online tech communities

Dear new developer,

Part of your job is keeping up to date with new technologies and happenings in the tech world. This can be a distraction because there are tools and techniques being released every day. Companies release new platforms, people publish interesting articles, and open source contributors release new tools. I avoid this distraction by relying on a community to filter the noise. To have an effective one, I had to find the right community.

If you know the precise technology on which you wish to focus, such as React Native or Haskell, sign up for an email list related to it. Find where the project is hosted and sign up for notifications. You can follow project contributors on Twitter or other social media sites. Matt Raible, a prolific developer and blogger,[1] once mentioned that he learns a new technology by unfollowing everyone in his Twitter feed. Then he follows only people connected to the new technology—his Twitter feed is therefore full of exactly what he needs to know.

However, if you aren't sure exactly what to focus on, a more general community might be a better fit. These are usually websites, but can be Slacks, forums, IRC channels, Facebook groups, or other means of online communication. These communities ebb and flow in popularity over the years. If you join a community and a few years later it is not as active or the feel has changed, look around. Chances are there is an up-and-coming community you can jump to.

Slashdot was the first online community I ever took part in. I enjoyed the discussions and open source focus. Most recently, I've moved to Hacker News, which has a mix of technology, science, business, and politics which I enjoy. But there are many other options available:

- Reddit, where you can find any type of community you want, from those focused on a specific technology like /r/oauth to those with a broad purview such as /r/programming

- Stack Overflow and the other Stack sites

- lobste.rs, which is less business and more technology focused

- HangOps, a Slack just for DevOps practitioners; it's one of many free, tech focused Slacks

Whatever community you join, make sure you actually *join the community*. Just as much of the value of a meetup is in who you see meeting after meeting, visiting an online community once is unlikely to be worthwhile. Be wary of self-promotion and seek guidance from the community on expectations if you have something to share. Take part in the community by commenting on posts, submitting interesting links, and in general being around.

Prepare to be offended or hurt by comments, especially if you say something not in line with community expectations. I have said dumb things. When I was called out for such behavior, I felt a flush of shame. I had to close the browser and get some space from the community for a time. In some cases, I've apologized. Doing so is no fun, but acknowledging your mistakes is part of the package when you join a community.

---

[1] He blogs at https://raibledesigns.com/

The more pleasant part of being a community member is the exposure to new ideas, technologies, and practices. You may want to discuss using a new technology or piece of open source software at work. Your employer may have policies around this, but it never hurts to ask. You also may discover new perspectives on technologies you are already using. Sharing articles or how-tos from the online community with your colleagues can help the team too. However, don't take every article shared on such sites as absolute truth; these communities often have a bias toward the exciting new thing.

It is also fun to submit a link or story, whether an interesting open source project, a blog post of your own, or an article you've run across. I've done that a few times, and it's a rush when my submission trends. It's also a nice way to say "thank you" to the author, and it only takes 30 seconds.

Find an online community, participate in it, and you will reap the rewards.

Sincerely,

Dan

You get what you give

Rylan Bowers is a developer, co-organizer of Boulder Startup Week and the Boulder Ruby Meetup, and an all-around good guy.

Dear new developer,

"You get what you give" isn't just a late 1990s catchy pop song set in a late 1990s mall that gives me a late 1990s cringe (and nostalgia, but those go hand in hand, eh?). It's also a great way to approach your career! This is something core to the tech scene I've adopted in Boulder, Colorado, as codified by Techstars with their Give First rule in their Code of Conduct.[2] Their other rules are great ones to build your career around, too.

I have found that giving provides many benefits to the giver:

- Offering to help engenders a greater sense of observation and consideration of others' needs and feelings. This is something we all can work on, given our reputation as social introverts.

- It feels good to help others with no strings attached.

- If you want to attach (small) strings for your own motivation, you increase how others view you in a positive light.

---

[2]https://www.techstars.com/code-of-conduct/

- You likely will find rewarding hobbies, coding interests, or other intrinsic rewards without much effort.

- You become less arrogant.

- You help build your community in a positive way, no matter how small the give is.

- People are quicker to recommend you for a job or position if you ever fall on harder times.

- It improves your own sense of self-worth and confidence.

- You make more friends outside of work.

- Did I mention that it just feels good?

My one caveat: There are always people who will take advantage; do try to be open-minded and kind, but watch out for takers, they will burn you out! Thankfully, they are few and far between.

Another great example of this mindset is Jason Cole's "Year of Giving Dangerously."[3] I must add that this way of living is out of reach for you as a new developer, but something to keep in mind over the course of your career. Give in small ways until you can give in bigger ways!

Also, be aware that being seen as only a taker is not a good thing. See my caveat earlier and think back on any time in your life that you've run into one. Maybe someone who always wanted to copy your answers or homework, but never contributed? Or those group projects where you felt like you were doing all the work? Don't be a taker.

Volunteer in your community. Be the good you want to see in the world.

—Rylan

Build your work community

Dear new developer,

Networking isn't just about meeting strangers and having conversations easily. Foster your community of former colleagues too. Doing so will help you if you are looking to hire, learn more about a potential employer, or ask questions about a software package. Here are some tips to help you maintain and foster your work connections.

---

[3]https://medium.com/@WickedSmaht/my-year-of-giving-dangerously-3ba44b3562ce

Use LinkedIn. Keep your profile up to date with your positions and accomplishments, as well as use it to connect with people you have met in a professional context.

Never leave a job on bad terms. Give the requisite notice, document your work, and prepare for a handoff. Don't speak ill of your former employer. You may be excited about the new job, but think about how you are leaving your current position. Treat your teammates as you'd want to be treated if they were departing.

Reach out periodically. This can be as simple as sending former coworkers a LinkedIn note when they have a work anniversary or have changed jobs. If you know they are interested in a technology and have run across an article on the topic, send it to them with a quick note. If you are visiting where they live, suggest meeting up for a coffee or beer.

If someone in your network has a request, try to help. Depending on the strength of the relationship, you may want to reshare the request, think of someone who could help, or volunteer yourself. Make sure your effort is proportional to the intensity of your connection. One time, I was overly enthusiastic about a new service an acquaintance was starting. I sent a bunch of intro emails for them. The service didn't end up succeeding, and I felt foolish for having overextended myself.

If you make a request, follow up when someone provides aid. Thank them and let them know how it helped. It feels great when you realize your assistance benefited someone. Don't ask for it too often from the same person, though. Spread around your requests. The stronger the relationship, the more often you can ask.

If you take care of your work network, when you want to tap it, former coworkers will respond. I've had former coworkers offer intros to interesting companies, provide contract work, and help me find the right hire.

Sincerely,

Dan

Three mantras to live by

Dave Mayer *is a long-time community building advocate, and by day he's CEO of Technical Integrity, a boutique recruiting firm focused on building diverse executive and technical teams for startups in Colorado and beyond.*

Dear new dev-

After 20+ years of "production level" experience in the real world, I'm writing to share three mantras that have led to more happiness and more success for us.

To be clear, these are DAILY mantras. Not weekly, not monthly, not annually. Daily.

They are:

- Surround yourself with people smarter than you.
- Build community and give without expecting anything in return.
- Listen to your gut, without exception.

Surround yourself every-damn-day with people who are smarter than you

You'll never be, nor should you, be the smartest person in the room. Confucius reportedly wrote "if you are the smartest person in the room, you're in the wrong room." Regardless of who wrote those words, they couldn't be truer. Since high school, I've always known that I was smart, but I was also clear that I was not the best at everything and that everyone had something to help me learn or to help me become a better student or a better human.

I'm not suggesting you surround yourself with jerks with a ton of pretense who can't stop talking about themselves and how smart they are; I'm suggesting that you learn to say "I don't know," "wow, that's cool, tell me more," and "yes, I could use some help." Knowing that you will never have all the answers, that it's okay to ask for help, and having an insatiable curiosity about engineering, life, music, and anything that is important to you will get you far in life.

Build community and give without expecting anything in return

In 2006, going into the "Great Recession," we sat in the back of the room at the Boulder-Denver New Tech Meetup and listened to Brad Feld talk about bringing people together and building community (in whatever area and subject that matters to you) with no expectation of anything in return. This idea of #GivingFirst was revolutionary to us 13 years ago, and it's been a life changer for us. It's a super simple yet elegant idea of walking into a room and asking how you can help someone solve their biggest challenges rather than where-do-they-work-or-what-kind-of-car-do-they-drive.[4] It's truly been life-changing to help others and embrace that as a BUSINESS philosophy, not just

---

[4]We wrote a detailed article, "Giving First Changed My Life", about this topic for *CTO Lunches* magazine, available here: https://newsstand.joomag.com/en/cto-quarterly-winter-2019/0598490001549481323

a life philosophy. It will all come back to you; you just don't know how or when, and that's okay.

Listen to your gut, every day without exception

It sounds simple, but not everyone does it. Your intuition is always right, yet folks second-guess themselves, rethink things, and question their own motivations. That's all healthy, and yes, you should "sleep on it," whatever "it" is. Space gives clarity. In large decisions, I ALWAYS take at least 24 hours to think on what the right answer is for me and to listen to my gut. It's NEVER failed me and it will never fail you. I promise.

I hope you will consider even one of these three mantras. You won't be disappointed.

—Dave

Build a personal board of advisors

Dear new developer,

You should build a board of advisors. For a startup, advisors are people with an informal relationship to the organization. They have not necessarily invested money but are available to help with issues that arise during the building of the business. At a new company, you want some advisors with experience in the area of business the company is pursuing. You also want variety—some with deep technology expertise, some who have a finance background, some with marketing experience.

In a similar fashion, I've found a personal board of advisors helpful. I've never formally asked the members to join, but there are three to four people to whom I reach out when I have a career issue. They are often former work colleagues who I respected and enjoyed. But they've also been people I've met at a meetup or conference.

When I need to discuss an issue, I tap people who have relevant experience. Here are some examples of problems I've discussed:

- I had a direct report who was not succeeding in their role.

- I had an issue with my manager that I wasn't sure how to solve.

- I was evaluating job offers.

The common thread is that these are specific, bounded problems hard to discuss frankly with my coworkers. Whether that's because you are concerned about rumors, have few peers, or are just seeking an outside perspective, a board of advisors is helpful. In particular, I would never discuss job offers with anyone at my current employer, yet they require thought and consultation.

Technology advice, on the other hand, should be sought from your team. They have the most context, and technology discussions shouldn't be risky in the same way as the preceding topics. But if you're new to your career, having someone outside of your work that is an expert in a technology you use on the job may help you understand the technology's strengths and weaknesses. This is especially true if you don't have anyone on your team with the time or expertise to help.

The value of this board of advisors is in the questions they ask and the context they have. One of my advisors, when I was talking about having left a company, mentioned it had seemed like a place I wasn't happy. He'd gleaned that through conversations and emails, and hearing him say that reminded me of my misery.

You don't need to talk with these folks on a regular schedule, but checking in every quarter keeps that context fresh. If they are in the same area, buy them coffee or a beer. Look for ways you can provide value to them; ask what you can do to help them, as they may be facing a problem that you have insight into, or perhaps you know someone they should chat with.

When you have a conversation, be explicit about the level of confidentiality. If I'm sharing something private, I say "can we keep this between us?" You need to trust anyone who acts as an advisor to you.

However, there is no need to be formal. Someone can be both a friend and an advisor, sometimes in the same hour. The list of people fulfilling this role will change as your needs change. When you are a new developer, you have different questions and challenges than you do when you are a team lead.

Building a board of advisors will help you when you run into an issue you can't discuss with your team but on which you require perspective.

Sincerely,

Dan

In conclusion

Community takes many forms. But all of them involve you, as a new developer, building relationships with other human beings. These relationships have been instrumental to my career success but are valuable beyond that. They've helped me help others. They've helped me in times of need and frustration. They've helped me talk through problems I was facing. They've helped me grow. A friend called community "the most powerful force in [his] career, hands down."

You are already a community member—unless you live on a desert island, I suppose. Be thoughtful and intentional about how you foster connections, help others, and participate.

Index

A

ActiveRecord, 73
Advice, 177, 178
Assuming negative intent, 88, 89
Automate business processes, 110
Automated testing, 65–67
awk, 57

B

Benchmarking, 71, 72
Big O notation, 131
Bizarre function, 59
Blogging
  benefits, 47
  commit to writing, 48
  feedback, 49
  like-minded interests, 47
  ongoing curiosity, 47
  online communities, 49
  plan, 50
  start, 47
  visitors and posts, 48
Board of advisors, 208, 209
Books, software, 142
Bootstrapped business,
  building, 117, 119
Brag document, 185, 186
Businesses

bootstrapped business building,
  guidelines, 117, 119
constraints and invisible structures, 105
developers fit, 114–116
goals and methods, 106
hammer, 116, 117
learn from customers, 119–121
no company is a monolith, 113, 114
outcomes over output, 108, 109
process crystallization, 109, 110
software is about people, 106, 107
spend money to make money, 110, 111
writing code, 107
Business model, 111–113
Business problems solving, 77, 79
Business process, selling custom
  software, 109

C

Career
  adaptable and authentic, 186
  advice, 177, 178
  brag document, writing, 185, 186
  contracting, 192, 193
  engineering management, 193–195
  layoff, 188–190
  learning over earning, 161, 162
  LinkedIn profile, setting up, 191, 192
  management
    communication, 180
    knowledge, 179
    progress, 180, 181

D. Moore, *Letters to a New Developer*, https://doi.org/10.1007/978-1-4842-6074-6

Printed in the United States
By Bookmasters